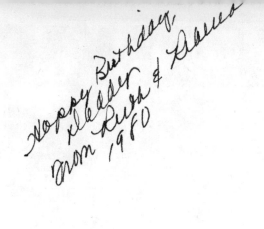

Happy Birthday,
Meredith
from Ruth & James
1980

ROMAN BRITAIN
OUTPOST OF THE EMPIRE

H. H. SCULLARD

ROMAN BRITAIN

OUTPOST OF THE EMPIRE

125 illustrations
5 maps

THAMES AND HUDSON

Maps on pp. 24, 36, 92, 112, 129
and line drawings on pp. 52, 139 and 169,
were drawn by Peter Bridgewater.

Library of Congress Catalog
card number 78–63042

Printed in the
United States of America

Contents

Preface

Another book on Roman Britain? Despite the number of existing works, a concise, up-to-date account may well be needed by the general reader, if only because of the speed with which archaeological discovery leads to the reassessment or illumination of existing views. Within the last decade new light has been thrown on the dating of the abandonment of both Hadrian's and the Antonine Walls, and of the building of the forts of the Saxon Shore. The early development of the Roman military and civil settlements at London and Colchester has been revealed; the discovery of new forts illustrates the stages of the Roman conquest of the west Midlands and southern Scotland, and the defensive measures taken on the Cumbrian coast. Other fresh aspects include: a great variety of new sites revealed by air photography; the headquarters of the British navy at Dover and the adjacent 'Painted House'; the writing-tablets found at Vindolanda, and an analysis of the diet of the Roman army; possible evidence of Christianity at Manchester in the late second century; the magnificent Christian silverware of Water Newton; the sculptured stones of the Thames-side monument and the quays; evidence for a temple of Isis in London; more inscriptions, including 162 lead scrolls containing curses; more graffiti, including one by a workman who broke 51 tiles, another seemingly mentioning a veterinary physician; more opticians' prescriptions. All these and more discoveries, made within the last ten years, help to amplify or modify our knowledge of the 400 years when Celtic and Roman cultures were learning to live together.

I am not unaware of the dangers of attempting this task, namely the inevitable dogmatism and oversimplification that a 'concise history' compels, together with all the risks that a mere historian of Rome must incur in venturing into a field of study that has become so highly specialized. However, I cannot help feeling that a short introductory book of this scope and scale may be needed, and I have at least tried to follow the best leaders, though unfortunately I can hardly acknowledge my numerous debts in any detail. I have drawn on a wide field and here I can mention only a few names with gratitude: A. Birley, A. R. Burn, R. G. Collingwood, S. S. Frere, J. Liversidge, T. G. Powell, I. A. Richmond, A. L. Rivet, J. M. C. Toynbee, J. Wacher and R. J. A. Wilson.

London, February 1978.   H. H. S.

Britain and the Celts

THE LAND AND ITS EARLY PEOPLES

Some 2,300 years ago an intrepid Greek sea captain and astronomer, Pytheas of Massilia (Marseilles), sailed out from the Mediterranean into the storm-tossed northern Atlantic. His first landfall in Britain was at Land's End, Cornwall. Here he observed how the natives skilfully mined tin, which they smelted and knocked into a knucklebone shape. After transporting it in boats made of wickerwork and sewn round with hides, they carried it at low tide in wagons across to the adjacent island of Ictis (St Michael's Mount) to meet foreign traders. So far Pytheas had only followed a trade route which went back to prehistoric times and had been exploited by Phoenicians, Carthaginians and perhaps some early Greeks. But he then went on to circumnavigate the British Isles: this was pioneering exploration of the first order, and his report gave the contemporary Greek world its first real knowledge of these islands.

Unfortunately his original account does not survive, and we have only a few extracts preserved by later writers. They record that Pytheas remarked on the height of the tides and their relation to the moon, and observed that Britain had a chilly climate and was thickly populated. The natives lived a primitive life in huts of wattle or wood, kept their corn in underground silos, ground what grain they needed, and brewed a drink from corn and honey. They had many kings and rulers, who generally lived in mutual peace, but when they did fight they used chariots. In the north of Scotland Pytheas heard about the distant land of Thule, the 'sleeping-place of the sun . . . near the frozen sea' (Iceland or Norway?) and later saw Ireland. He believed the British Isles to be triangular, and though his reckoning of the total of their sides (4,675 miles) is considerably exaggerated, he was a good astronomer who calculated the latitude of Massilia with the greatest accuracy, and appears to have been a reliable reporter despite the doubts expressed by many ancient writers.

After this tantalizing glimpse the British Isles disappeared for some time from the sight of the Greek and Roman world, partly because the Carthaginians gained firmer control of the western Mediterranean and barred the Atlantic at the Straits of Gibraltar to all foreign shipping. Then, after the fall of Carthage in 146 BC, any traders from the Mediterranean who sailed to Britain were interested only in Cornish tin and did not penetrate inland. Nor did a Roman, P. Crassus, who reached Cornwall early in the first century BC. Thus for some two centuries after Pytheas, Britain remained a land of mystery. In 55 BC, when Julius Caesar planned to attack the island, he had to gather first-hand information from cross-Channel traders in northern

Opposite, pre-Roman Britain: Maiden Castle near Dorchester, a stronghold and sanctuary from the Neolithic till the Iron Age, and one of the most dramatic sites in Britain.

France, and from an officer whom he had sent across to reconnoitre. But even after two brief campaigns in the southeast, Caesar's knowledge of the island remained limited and in part defective.

The history of man is obviously governed in the last resort by his own actions, but the physical formation of a country profoundly affects the pattern and history of its early settlement. This is particularly true in Britain with its sharp division into a highland and lowland area, marked geologically by the Jurassic ridge from Flamborough Head in Yorkshire to Plymouth Hoe in Devonshire. The inhospitable mountains of the north and west, with their hard rocks, poorer soil, and higher rainfall, made communications difficult and discouraged settlement, whereas the lowland zone in the south and east provided a gentler climate, more fertile land, and easier communications, at least along the river valleys and the trackways on the ridges of the lower hills, cutting through the widespread forests. In addition, the lowlands faced continental Europe, notably the coastlands from the Rhine delta to Brittany, and were more open to invasion: hence the perennial tendency for waves of invaders to try to master the southeast. The Romans were no exception: they overran and civilized the more open country, which became the heart of 'Roman Britain', and then had to withstand pressure from the inhabitants of the wilder country beyond.

Man's development in Britain, from the builders of such megalithic structures as Stonehenge down to the late Iron Age folk whom Caesar encountered when he invaded the island in. 55 BC, is a fascinating, if sometimes confused, story. Society in the later part of the Bronze Age (roughly 1400–700 BC) remained fairly static; its patterns of settlement, burial customs and pottery did not change much. But in the eighth century there was a quickening of activity, especially in bronzeworking, due to increasing trade and the import of foreign goods. Gradually Iron Age cultures emerged, but they were rooted in the earlier period. The history of the Iron Age in Britain used to be conveniently divided into three cultural stages, with increasing subdivision and refinement as archaeology provided more and more material. These stages, *A, B* and *C*, were related to postulated invasions of Celtic peoples from the Continent from the seventh to the early first century, and they were linked to the cultural development of the continental Celts (of the so-called Hallstatt, La Tène I and II, and La Tène III periods, which were named after typical sites in Austria and Switzerland).

Julius Caesar recorded that some of the Belgae, a tribe which occupied the lands in France north of the Seine and Marne, had settled in the coastal areas of southern Britain. Although he gave no date for this invasion, which theoretically *could* have been centuries before his time, it probably took place not long before. Some archaeologists are now very doubtful whether *earlier* cultural changes need have been caused by widespread invasions rather than by commercial contacts and the differentiation of local pottery types. Thus it is argued that from the mid-eighth to the mid-fourth century there was lively trading with the Continent. When this died down during the third and second centuries, regional differences increased among the British communities until renewed contact was made with the Continent following the arrival of Belgic settlers towards the end of the second century.

Whatever the precise origins, be they widespread invasions or the gradual infiltration of ideas and goods, Celtic culture steadily spread in the lowland zone of Britain from the sixth century BC onwards, though the highland zone was largely still occupied by peoples leading an almost Bronze Age pastoral life when the Romans arrived. This Celtic culture derived from a Bronze Age people of the Upper Danube, often called the Urnfield people because they buried the ashes of their dead in urns deposited in large cemeteries. It emerged when they were amalgamated with a warrior aristocracy coming from the east, and developed the use of iron. Hence it radiated outwards into northern Italy, Spain, France and Britain. Although thus diffused, it remained a recognizable unitary culture through its use of a common speech, social structure, religion and artistic traditions. We shall look at some of these wider aspects shortly, but first we must see what picture the archaeological evidence provides for settlement in Britain.

Like their predecessors, the Celts in Britain were an agricultural people, living in farmsteads or village groupings among the fields that they cultivated. Their field system was derived from Bronze Age or even Neolithic usage. These so-called 'Celtic fields' were rectangular (unlike the Saxon strip-fields), and traces of them still survive on chalk downlands, marked out by banks or lynchets which were formed on sloping ground when soil was disturbed by ploughing higher up and then swept downwards to the lower edges of the field. The plough, which was probably drawn by a pair of oxen,

Celtic fields at Smacam Down, Dorset. Rectangular in shape, these may derive from a system dating back to the New Stone Age.

was an 'ard' which lacked a mould-board to turn the sods, and so could cut only a light furrow. The harvested grain was roasted and stored in the farmstead, either in timber granaries with raised floors or in deep pits. Pigs and goats, as well as cattle and sheep, had been domesticated. Spinning and weaving were conducted at home. Pottery was also still a home craft, and not yet made on a wheel. Thus the farms were largely self-supporting, except for metals, which were sold to them by itinerant traders. From about 500 BC iron mainly superseded bronze for common use. However, from the fourth century some specialization developed, and good quality pottery was produced at certain centres for distribution over a neighbouring area for sale.

The inhabited area of a settlement was generally enclosed by a palisaded enclosure or an earth bank. Hundreds of such farmsteads, spanning several centuries, have been traced. One of the best-known later examples is at Little Woodbury, just south of Salisbury, which flourished about 400–100 BC. Here an early palisaded enclosure was replaced by a bank and ditch which protected some four acres. Within was a massive circular hut, about 45 feet in diameter, together with another smaller building, overground granaries and slightly later storage pits for grain. Many bones of animals survive, together with evidence of the inhabitants' pottery-making, weaving and use of querns.

Beside these smaller settlements, which might occasionally be combined to form a slightly larger community, some considerable plateau enclosures existed to serve for tribal meetings. From about 600 BC some of these were strengthened by ramparts and ditches, and developed into hillforts, and by 400 BC they had become very numerous. A number were thereafter abandoned, but others were fortified even more strongly, occupying an average area of some 10–20 acres and sometimes containing rows of houses. They thus formed bases for local leaders, each of whom may have gained control of some 30–40 square miles. Society was changing, and tribal groups started to form for defence or attack, with the peasant cultures beginning to show more aristocratic features which were reflected in the variety and increase of these hillforts. This development from the fairly simple structures of the fifth and fourth centuries into the complex defences of *c.* 100 BC can well be traced at such sites as Maiden Castle in Dorset and Danebury in Hampshire. The use of the long sword and war chariot also developed. At the same time, in response to the needs of an emerging warrior aristocracy, new artistic features appeared. These reflected the lively art of the La Tène period, with its non-representational forms and patterns and its interlocking scrolls, which now decorated both domestic pottery and the splendid metalwork of the rich chieftains. But if hillforts and inter-tribal warfare, conducted by powerful new leaders, were changing some aspects of society, life in the countryside farms continued in its older ways.

Then in the decades about 100 BC Belgic tribes began to settle in southeast Britain; the approximate date is shown by the fact that in Kent and Essex types of Gallo-Belgic coinage have been found which originated in the area of the Somme between 150 and 100 BC. The coins also reveal a complicated pattern of settlement. The existing Celtic population resisted stoutly and strengthened some of their hillforts: thus the east gate at Danebury was massively refortified but was later burned down by the invaders, while at

Worlebury in Somerset the decapitated bodies of some of the attackers, buried near the entrances, bear witness to the struggle. In their attempts to carve out tribal kingdoms for themselves the Belgic leaders clearly met with continued resistance from the local rulers as they thrust westwards. During the early years of conflict they often made use of the existing hillforts which they captured, but the strongholds (*oppida*) which they themselves built were large and constructed on lower ground. We have here reached a point where archaeology and written history can provide joint testimony. Caesar records that the *oppidum* of Cassivellaunus, who established his rule in Hertfordshire, was defended by woods and marshes and was large enough to hold many men and cattle: 'The Britons call it an *oppidum* when they have fortified thickly wooded places with a rampart and ditch, as a place to assemble in order to avoid the attacks of their enemies.' Cassivellaunus' *oppidum* can almost certainly be identified with the fort at Wheathampstead, where the earthworks enclose an area of some 90–100 acres, thus making it the size of a small town by Romano-British standards.

Elsewhere Caesar gives his general impression of Britain. This is curiously defective on some points, but it must be remembered that his two visits were extremely brief, and were devoted to military operations in the southeast only:

The interior is inhabited by peoples who according to their own oral tradition are indigenous, the coast by peoples who had crossed over from Belgium to plunder and

The British Celtic hillfort was a rallying point for the dispersed population. Here Maiden Castle, seen from the air, reveals successive stages of development from plateau enclosure to complex defence system.

make war. Nearly all the latter retain the names of the tribes from which they had originated [e.g. the Atrebates of Arras and Berkshire]; after the invasion they settled down and began to till the soil. The population is exceedingly large, the homesteads very near together and closely resembling those of the Gauls, and the cattle very numerous. For money they use either bronze or gold coins, or iron ingots of fixed weight. Tin is found inland, and small quantities of iron near the coast; the copper they use is imported. There is timber of every kind, as in Gaul, except beech and fir. They think it wrong to eat hares, fowl and geese, but they rear them for interest and pleasure. The climate is more temperate than in Gaul, the cold being less severe.

By far the most civilized inhabitants are those in Kent (a purely maritime district), whose way of life differs very little from that of the Gauls. Most of the tribes of the interior do not grow corn but live on milk and meat and wear skins. All the Britons dye themselves with woad, which produces a blue colour and makes their appearance in battle more frightening. They wear their hair long and shave the whole of their bodies except the head and the upper lip. Wives are shared between groups of ten or twelve men, especially between brothers and between fathers and sons; but the offspring of these unions are reckoned as the children of the man with whom a particular woman first cohabited.

Caesar has here clearly underestimated the general level of culture, more details of which will be discussed later. But in passing we may just note that tin was in fact mined only in Cornwall, not 'inland', and copper was worked at an early date in the West Country; beech forests existed in Britain from the earliest times; corn was grown even in the Neolithic Age; and woollen and linen clothes were certainly used before Caesar; the application of woad was presumably restricted to battle, if painted on the body, though the reference may be to tattooing; and finally polyandry may have survived in remote districts, but it was not a Celtic custom.

THE CELTS

Thus a Celtic culture, which absorbed certain elements of the earlier population, developed in Britain to the time of Caesar. Since these Celts remained the foundation of the population throughout the long years of Roman occupation, and since the interaction between their native civilization and that of Rome forms one of the main topics of this book, we should now examine some further aspects of Celtic life. Caesar, as well as other classical writers, has much to tell about the Gauls in France and elsewhere, and this information has been greatly extended by archaeological research.

All Celts spoke dialects of a common language belonging to the Indo-European group of tongues, which included Greek and Latin. In the British Isles the main dialects were Goedelic (Irish, Scottish Gaelic and Manx) and Brythonic (Welsh, Cornish and Breton). Like most early peoples, the Celts were essentially illiterate and, in the absence of writing, the spoken word was supreme; thus, as Caesar noted, they relied on the training of the memory to preserve their traditions and ways of life. This led to the development of oratory and poetry, a tradition that survived even until the later Roman empire; Symmachus, for instance, the great orator of the fourth century AD, was trained by a rhetorician from Gaul.

The physical appearance of the Celts is revealed in skeletal remains, in representations in plastic art and, above all, in descriptions given by classical writers, who were greatly struck by their height, fair skin, blue eyes and blond hair, so different from the shorter, darker men of the Mediterranean world. Celtic graves often contain remains of both long-headed and round-headed men, and it may be assumed that the former represent the Celtic type, the latter the descendants of the older Bronze Age population. So in Britain both types lived together, but the chieftains and warriors were drawn from the tall, fair, long-headed men who impressed and terrified the Greeks and the Romans in battle. The nobles grew long moustaches but otherwise were clean-shaven, and the warriors stiffened their hair into quills with lime. The appearance of the Celtic invaders of Italy at the battle of Telamon in 225 BC is vividly recorded by the historian Polybius, who describes how they rushed into battle on foot or horseback, or in chariots, some naked, some in trousers and light cloaks; their iron weapons, long swords, high stature, streaming hair, weird cries, blaring horns and trumpets, flashing gold torcs (necklaces) and bracelets, terrified even the disciplined Roman legionaries, until superior weapons and better battle tactics finally gave the Romans the victory.

The Celts' everyday dress probably consisted of a tunic and cloak, fastened by a safety-pin brooch, for both sexes. Diodorus comments on their coloured cloaks, dyed and embroidered shirts, and gold or silver decorated belts. Splendid ornaments, especially torcs of gold or bronze, were worn by those men and women who could afford such luxury. 'The Gauls,' wrote Timagenes in the late Roman republic, 'are all exceedingly careful of cleanliness and neatness, nor in all the country . . . could any man or woman, however poor, be seen either dirty or ragged'. There are references to special soaps and perfumes for women, but these apply to a time when Gauls had

The torc, a characteristically Celtic ornament worn by both men and women: this fine example in gold was found at Snettisham, Norfolk, homeland of the Iceni tribe.

long been in contact with the civilized world of Rome. An earlier period is covered by Strabo, writing in the time of Augustus, who reported that the whole Celtic nation was war⁄mad 'and both high⁄spirited and quick for battle, although otherwise simple and not uncouth'.

The Celts were living in a 'heroic' age, when personal bravery in battle, even recklessness, was accounted the highest virtue. They loved feasting and quarrelling, praise and boasting, personal adornment and bright colours. Poseidonius, writing in the late Roman republic, describes a Celtic chieftain named Lovernius and his love of feasting: 'When at length he fixed a day for the ending of the feast, a Celtic poet who arrived too late met Lovernius and composed a song magnifying his greatness and lamenting his own late arrival. Lovernius was very pleased and asked for a bag of gold and threw it to the poet who ran beside his chariot. The poet picked it up and sang another song.' The Celts also exhibited some savage traits, including drunkenness, human sacrifice and head⁄hunting. Adventurous yet fickle, they lacked staying power and after battle quickly scattered to plunder or enjoy their spoil. But in general they were both adaptable and hospitable, and maintained a fairly stable social structure within the tribe.

This was the social unit, and tribe warred against tribe. The centre, as we have seen, was the hillfort which formed a rallying point for a dispersed rural population. The Celts were not town⁄dwellers, and urbanization was a way of life that came to many of them only through the later ordering of Rome. Although among many Celtic tribes aristocracy, based on the tie between noble overlords and large bodies of client retainers, had replaced kingship, among the Belgae kings still ruled. According to Caesar, Gaulish society was divided into three groups: the Druids, the warrior aristocracy (*Equites* or Knights), and the common people. The Druids, who were in fact drawn from the warrior class, ranked highest. They were priests who controlled all public and private sacrifices, which might include human victims, and they judged nearly all disputes, whether between tribes or between individuals; they were also exempt from military service and taxation. Their leaders were chosen by election or by armed combat. They were concerned not only with religious and semi⁄magical duties, but also with regulating seasonal festivals and educating the sons of the leaders. They shared wealth and political power with the nobles, who rivalled one another in the number of their retainers, both freemen and slaves. The rest of the people consisted largely of free cultivators, but the condition of many must have been wretched, some sinking to serfdom or even slavery.

The Celtic family was patriarchal, and its head had absolute power over all his household. Celtic women, no less than their menfolk, seem to have impressed classical writers. Diodorus records that like their men they were not only great in stature but also their equals in courage, while Ammianus Marcellinus, following Timagenes, noted that 'a whole band of foreigners would not be able to withstand a single Gaul if he called on the help of his wife, who is usually stronger than he and blue⁄eyed'. Though in early times women were probably debarred from holding independent property, they were soon allowed more freedom. On occasion the regal authority was vested in a woman, such as Boudicca and Cartimandua in Roman times, while

A Gallic calendar from Coligny, France, illustrates the sophisticated Druidic calendrical system, based on the moon, with the month divided into 'bright' and 'dark' halves. The holes at left were for pegs to mark feast days.

much earlier (*c.* 400 BC?) a princess of obvious importance had been buried with great splendour at Vix in Burgundy. In fact funerals of the great were always costly, and Caesar said that people still alive in his day could remember the times when favourite slaves and retainers were burnt on their master's funeral pyre.

The Celts, like most early peoples, felt that supernatural or magical powers dominated all aspects of their lives and surroundings. The spirits of forest, river, mountain, sea and sky had to be pacified by ritual and sacrifice. Though a mythology existed, in early days these magical powers were not clearly differentiated, and each tribal group might have its own views about the gods. Such beliefs may to some extent have reflected the human social order, but only after contact with the Mediterranean world did these Celtic deities gain very precise and specific functions and attributes. Evidence from pre-Roman times is in fact very scanty, and it is difficult to isolate early beliefs from their later accretions. The contribution of both classical writers and later Irish and Welsh sources requires very critical application, as also does the contribution of archaeology. Some early wooden images survive in France, but little stone statuary: the interesting stone statues of warriors and human heads found near the mouth of the Rhône are not typically Celtic, but rather

Epona, the Celtic 'Great Mare' goddess.

Opposite, the White Horse at Uffington, a hill figure of probable Celtic origin, measures over 370 feet from nose to tail and illustrates the stylized nature of Celtic art.

Celtic adaptations of Graeco-Roman practice. However, they do testify to Poseidonius' report that it was the custom of the Gauls to nail the decapitated heads of their enemies to the doorposts of their houses. In fact human skulls found at a hillfort on Bredon Hill in Worcestershire may originally have decorated its gateway. This practice, however, was not mere trophy-hunting, but probably originated from magical practices concerned with fertility or subduing the ghosts of the dead.

The Celts in Britain may have believed in a great tribal god and a nature goddess who was his mate, but it was the local manifestation of these deities which was significant for the ordinary man. We know the names of many gods which were recognized and worshipped in very limited areas. Some deities tended to be worshipped in groups of three, or sometimes in single form. Thus Epona (the Great Mare), who is generally shown riding on a horse, is found in both triple and single form. It is uncertain whether she should be connected with the great White Horse cut out in the chalk hillside 500 feet above the Thames valley at Uffington in Berkshire, but this may well be Celtic in origin, as may the giant figure carved on the hill of Cerne Abbas

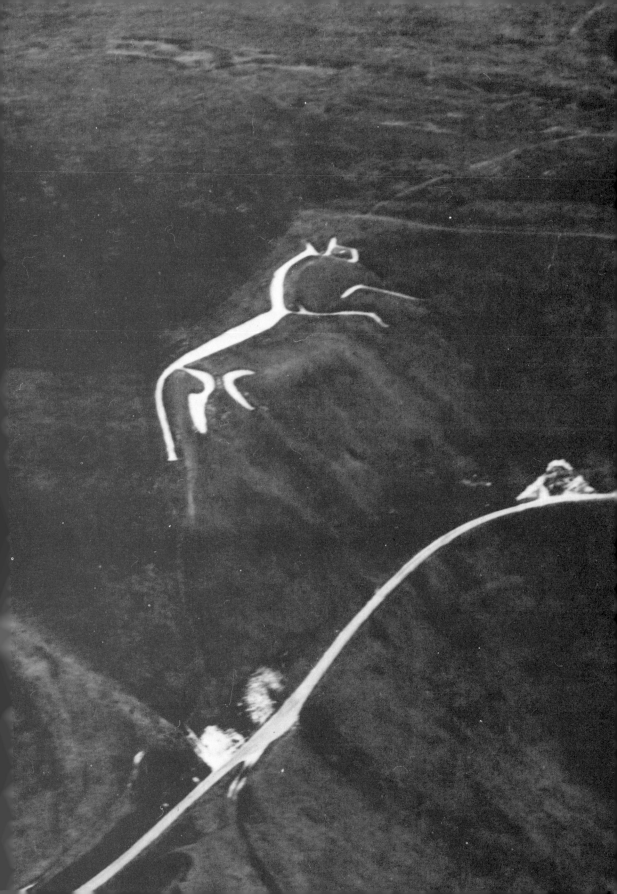

in Dorset (though since he is depicted with a club he may be Romano-British and assimilated to the Roman Hercules). Epona appears at times to have been identified with one of the nature goddesses, the *Deae Matronae*. These too are often grouped in threes, although they sometimes appear singly and may be given a special name, such as Rosmerta. The spirit who presided over a local spot, such as a well, spring, tree or grove, might remain nameless (the genius or spirit of the place: *genius loci* in later Roman phraseology); or it might be personified and named, as with Coventina, a nymph who presided over a spring outside the later Roman fort at Carrawburgh on Hadrian's Wall. In fact very many of these Celtic deities only took shape under Roman influences, as we shall see (pp. 157ff.), and their early forms remain very obscure, as indeed they probably often were in the minds of their worshippers.

The individual needed help in facing these uncertain powers, and this was provided by the Druids, the preservers of a sacred literature of myths, charms and incantations, and the regulators of all sacrifices. Their doctrine was handed down by oral tradition, being committed to memory since it was not allowed to be written. It included a belief in the immortality of the soul, which inculcated bravery and contempt of death. The Druids also reasoned about the nature of the world and the gods. Caesar believed that Druidic teaching originated in Britain and remained strongest there. He reported that the Druids in Gaul came together annually for a common meeting, and we can assume that the Druids in Britain had a similar organization. The system, therefore, formed a unifying (and at times an indirectly political) bond between the various tribes.

The Druids had no temples. Worship took place in sacred groves where the trees provided the holy precincts. Caesar also mentions human sacrifices, which sometimes took the form of burning men alive in large wickerwork cages. Prophecies might be formulated in accordance with the agonized movements of the victims.

The poet Lucan refers to three Celtic gods, Taranis, Teutates and Esus, who were apparently propitiated by the respective burning, drowning and hanging of sacrificial victims. In addition, the Druidic teaching was supplemented by bards and seers (*vates*; cf. Irish *fathi*), the latter possibly using trance states to 'see' into the future.

Brave at times to the point of bravado, the Celts lacked discipline in battle, and tribe often preferred to fight tribe rather than to cooperate against a common enemy. The war chariot, which in Gaul had been entirely superseded by cavalry in Caesar's day, survived in Britain. Caesar described its use in battle, and considered that it combined the mobility of cavalry with the stability of infantry. The chariots were deployed with great skill, being driven wildly along the enemy lines and accompanied by much noise and the discharge of missiles to cause confusion. The warriors could even stand on the draught pole and the yoke in order to seem more menacing. When they had worked their way through the squadrons of enemy cavalry, the warriors leapt down to fight on foot, while their charioteers withdrew to a safe spot in the distance to which their masters might retreat if forced back. In pre-Caesarian times perhaps some individual combats between chiefs may have preceded the main mêlée, but such heroic behaviour would not defeat disciplined

Taranis, a Celtic god
mentioned by the Roman
poet Lucan: a pottery mould
found at Corbridge
(Corstopitum) on Hadrian's
Wall.

Roman legionaries. The Britons' equipment included heavy broadswords
which could be used for cutting and slashing, but not for thrusting, and they
carried one or two spears, a long shield and sometimes a dagger.

If fighting against overseas invaders was a grim business, inter-tribal
warfare must at times have been more of a sport which was an essential part of
Celtic aristocratic life, and thus demanded above all splendid equipment. It
was the warrior's requirement for fine metalwork – bronze shields and sword-
scabbards, enamelled harness and snaffle-bits for the horses, and bronze
fittings for the chariots – that stimulated late Celtic art in Britain. The
essence of this art is that it was non-representational and avoided naturalism
and reproducing the human figure and straight lines. Rather it was abstract,

delighting in waving and curving lines and tendrils, often woven together into intricate patterns. It originated of course in the La Tène culture of continental Europe, and reached Britain by (at least) the mid-third century BC, when native schools developed in the island. It also received further stimulus with the arrival of the Belgae. At their best these artists produced such masterpieces as the bronze mirror from Birdlip, with its incised design of plant or scroll patterns, the bronze horned helmet from the Thames with its red enamel decoration, and the Battersea shield with embossed curvilinear decoration. Their art also found expression in the coinage which came into use in the first century BC. The continental Celts had imitated the coins of Philip II of Macedon which depicted the head of Apollo and, on the reverse, a two-horse chariot. Unable, or at any rate unwilling, to reproduce these realistic designs, the Celts of Gaul had split up the component features of the types and rearranged them in various decorative patterns. Beside their artistic interest, these Gallo-Celtic coins and those made in Britain provide valuable evidence for the spread of the Celtic tribes in Britain and for the later history of their dynasties, as well as indicating how under Roman influences many Celts began to abandon barter, first in Gaul and later in Britain. But although art in early Britain obviously represented the flowering of the Celtic spirit, we should remember that it was developed largely for the needs of an aristocracy and, therefore, was not so deeply rooted that its continuance at a high level was guaranteed when that demand declined.

Opposite, a Celtic masterpiece: bronze mirror with engraved back from the grave of a lady of the aristocracy at Birdlip, Glos.

Approximate tribal divisions
in Britain

1 Isurium (Aldborough)
2 Petuaria (Brough)
3 Ratae (Leicester)
4 Viroconium (Wroxeter)
5 Venta Icenorum
  (Caistor)
6 Venta Silurum
  (Caerwent)
7 Corinium (Cirencester)
8 Verulamium (St
  Albans)
9 Camulodunum
  (Colchester)
10 Isca (Exeter)
11 Durnovaria (Dorchester)
12 Calleva (Silchester)
13 Noviomagus
  (Chichester)
14 Durovernum
  (Canterbury)
15 Venta Belgarum
  (Winchester)

Caesar and the native kingdoms

Before he encountered Belgic tribes in Britain, Julius Caesar had defeated their Gallic cousins in France in 57 BC. The latter, as we have seen, comprised a confederation of warlike tribes in northeastern France, who had originally come over the Rhine from the east. Though, according to Caesar, they claimed to be of Germanic origin, they spoke a Celtic language and their chiefs at least had Celtic names, so they were probably of that race with perhaps some slight Teutonic intermixture. The Belgic tribes which crossed the Channel seized a large part of southern England, as various waves or groups of invaders arrived. Their main area of settlement probably included Kent, Hertfordshire, Buckinghamshire, east Hampshire, west Sussex and Berkshire, but individual chiefs may have extended their control over the earlier inhabitants to a somewhat wider extent. The Belgae may not have introduced the heavy plough, but their agriculture included better iron tools so that they could exploit the heavier soils. In addition, corn was stored in pottery jars rather than in silos.

The Belgae began to settle on lower ground at river crossings, and a number of these sites, unlike so many of the earlier hillforts, have continued to be inhabited ever since. Trade too increased, helped by the introduction of coinage, which gradually replaced the iron bars referred to by Caesar. The iron resources of the country, especially in the Weald, were exploited, and metal industries flourished, culminating in the artistry of such magnificent works as the Battersea shield and the gold torcs and bracelets from Snettisham in Norfolk. Pottery was now made on the wheel, and the dead were cremated; the ashes of the poor were placed in urns, while those of the rich were buried in elaborate tombs often covered by a barrow.

The Belgae were naturally interested in cross-Channel trade with their kinsmen in northeast France, while the tribes of southwest England were concerned to maintain contacts with northwestern France, where the seafaring Veneti of Brittany (Armorica) were the dominant power and controlled the old tin route to Cornwall. When Caesar advanced against the Veneti in 57 BC they submitted, but thoughts of Roman competition induced a quick change of mind: they revolted, and even sent for help to Britain. Caesar had a very tough campaign on his hands against their great Atlantic fleet, and their forts perched on cliff promontories. However, he won a victory in Quiberon Bay, and went on to reduce the tribe with great cruelty. Many tried to escape, and some reached southern England. Thus Caesar achieved naval supremacy in the Channel, and also knew that the Veneti as well as the Belgae had received help from fellow Celts in Britain.

The tribes of southern Britain now realized that they were lying dangerously poised on the edge of a great Mediterranean empire which, with the Roman conquest of France, actually faced them across the Channel. They also had reason to fear that Caesar might stage a punitive raid, if not a full-scale invasion. Luckily for them, however, Caesar, although needing military glory, also needed time to consolidate his conquest of France, while political conditions in Rome made it inadvisable for him to be away from Italy for too long. If he decided to attack Britain, he would have to act swiftly. This he did, partly for military reasons arising from the Gallic situation, partly perhaps in the hope of some economic gain since he had learnt of its mineral wealth, and partly to win a victory 'beyond the Ocean' which might help to counterbalance his rival Pompey's spectacular victories in the Caucasus and the East. Hence his two expeditions were glorified raids, which did not have to be pushed home if they ran into too many difficulties.

Having failed to extract much information about Britain from Gallic merchants, he sent an officer to reconnoitre and received envoys from some British tribes who promised to surrender on his arrival. In order to help pave his way, he sent back with these emissaries a Celt named Commius, whom he had previously installed as king of the Atrebates in Belgic Gaul. Commius was to bring as many British tribes into the Roman fold as he could, including perhaps the British Atrebates who may have been hostile to the Belgic tribes to their east. Commius failed, however, since he was arrested as soon as he arrived in the island.

On 26 August 55 BC Caesar launched some 10,000 men and 500 cavalry across the Channel from Boulogne (Gesoriacum) against the approaches to an island which Cicero, writing to his friend Atticus in the following year, described as 'walled around with amazingly great cliffs' (*aditus muratos mirificis molibus*). Finding the cliffs of Dover manned by defenders, he landed his forces on a shelving beach near Walmer and Deal, having failed in an earlier reconnaissance to find the safe harbour of Richborough (Rutupiae) a little further north. However, once ashore the legionaries routed the opposing Britons, and the chiefs in Kent submitted, even though Caesar could not follow up his success because storms were delaying the arrival of his cavalry. Near disaster followed when his ships, which in default of a harbour had been beached on the open shore, were wrecked by a storm, and a fresh fleet had to be improvised in the face of renewed hostility. But Caesar's luck held, and he managed to evacuate his forces and reach France before the autumn equinoctial gales, taking some British hostages with him. Reports sent to Rome minimized his setbacks and emphasized his solid successes: he *had* forced the barbarians across the Channel to surrender. Moreover, he had learnt how they fought and used their chariots, and how quickly they would surrender after a defeat; he also found that much grain was available in the southeast. So he determined on a larger expedition in the next year.

At nightfall on 6 July 54 BC, some 25,000 legionaries and 2,000 cavalry set sail from Boulogne in about 800 vessels and landed, this time unopposed, between Deal and Sandwich. Leaving his ships at anchor, Caesar defeated the assembled Britons near the Stour and then stormed their hillfort (Bigbury Hill, west of Canterbury). But the next day news came that his fleet had again been wrecked and driven on to shore. He had to return to supervise the start of the vast task of repairing the ships, and then left to resume the attack. The interval had allowed the Britons to rally under Cassivellaunus, king of the Belgic Catuvellauni, who ruled in the area of Hertfordshire, north of the Thames. Thrusting aside harassing chariot attacks, the Romans reached the Thames, which they crossed (probably at London, perhaps at Tilbury) with great courage, despite stakes fixed under the river and water up to their necks. Ahead lay great forests and further harassment by British chariots. Caesar, however, managed to gain the support of the Trinovantes in Essex, who asked him to instal as their king a prince named Mandubracius who had fled to Caesar in Gaul when his father had been murdered by Cassivellaunus. Other smaller tribes followed their example and surrendered. Caesar then launched his legionaries against Cassivellaunus' formidable *oppidum* (most probably at Wheathampstead), which they stormed. Meantime the king managed to persuade four Kentish chieftains to attack Caesar's naval camp in his rear, but this last throw failed and the attack was beaten off.

Both sides were now ready for peace: while Cassivellaunus would be glad to see the back of his unwelcome guest, Caesar had to leave before the autumn storms, and he was also worried about events in Gaul. Hostages were exacted, an annual tribute payable to the Roman people was agreed, and the Trinovantes were guaranteed immunity from Cassivellaunus' aggression. Two months after his first landing Caesar was back in Gaul; southeast Britain had been conquered and the foundations laid for further conquest if Caesar had the opportunity or Rome the will.

THE ATREBATES AND THE CATUVELLAUNI

Despite rumours of renewed invasions, Britain was in fact left largely to its own devices for almost 100 years between the invasions of Caesar and the emperor Claudius. A distant island like Britain could, and indeed had to, wait, when the whole structure of Roman government was changing. Civil wars led to the breakdown of the Roman republic, and Augustus emerged as the sole ruler of an empire which preserved the semi-illusory belief that he was the first citizen in a restored republic. Whatever they may have thought of their immediate future, the Britons of the southeast were at least more conscious of the power of Rome, to whom they now had to pay tribute, though it is uncertain how long this was regularly collected. Their external trade, especially in tin, suffered some temporary interruption, but thereafter commercial and cultural contacts with the Continent enabled some of the native kingdoms to develop into stronger political and social units, especially the Atrebates south of the Thames and the Catuvellauni north of the river. The evidence for the growth of these and other tribal areas is somewhat sparse and uneven: for their political history we depend largely upon their widespread and increasingly Romanized coinage, while for their social and economic progress, archaeological research has provided considerable material. The wider background is illuminated by a few scattered references in the writings of classical authors.

South of the Middle Thames Commius, Caesar's protégé, who had been set free, finally gained control of the Atrebates after many adventures. He had deserted his leader, supported the revolt of Vercingetorix in Gaul, survived two attempts at assassination, surrendered, and then escaped to Britain, where he created a strong kingdom among the Atrebates with its capital at Silchester (Calleva), and established a dynasty. His son Tincommius (who ruled from *c.* 25/20 BC to AD 5/6) managed to reach some agreement with Augustus about 16 BC, and later introduced a new coinage resembling that of Rome rather than that of his predecessors; he also imported more Roman pottery. We have what seem to be crude portraits of Tincommius and some other British rulers (namely his brothers Verica and Eppillus, the Catuvellaunian father and son Tasciovanus and Cunobelinus, and Dubnovellaunus and Adminius, who ruled in Kent). Their heads sometimes appear on their coinage, which was struck in gold, silver and bronze. Though their features and hairstyles sometimes resemble those of the emperors Augustus or Tiberius, they were probably meant to represent the British rulers, who thus asserted their aspirations to cultural parity with the Roman world. Tincommius' good relations with Rome were made possible by the turn which Augustus' policy took.

Augustus was the adopted son and successor of Julius Caesar, whose unfinished task of conquering Britain might be considered part of his legacy. Indeed, in the early part of his reign the court poets implied that he *would* thus add to his glory, and he was even said to have been on the point of launching an expedition on three occasions (in 34, 27, and 26 BC), only to be deterred by disturbances in Dalmatia, Gaul and Spain. However, if he ever in fact entertained the idea, it is clear that he gradually abandoned it. His contemporary, the geographer Strabo, pointed out that Britain was difficult of access and harmless to Rome, and more profitable as an independent source of trade than as a province (i.e. the customs dues levied on British exports would outweigh the revenue of a province requiring the expense of a large military garrison). Moreover, some British chiefs had submitted to Rome and had 'made the whole island almost a Roman country'.

Whatever may be thought of Strabo's reasons, Augustus may well have decided to allow the idea of an invasion of Britain to die a natural death, welcoming the approach of Tincommius as a means of ensuring a balance of rival powers within the island. Such an agreement also helped Tincommius later, since when he was expelled from his kingdom some time before AD 7, he was able to flee to Rome where he was received by Augustus. His downfall was apparently due to the treachery of his brother Eppillus who succeeded him: dynastic quarrels often weakened British tribes. Augustus accepted the situation and even allowed Eppillus to place the title REX on his coins. The new king, however, was soon expelled by another brother, Verica, who reigned until driven out in AD 43 after the aggressions of the Catuvellaunian king, Cunobelinus. Verica then fled to the emperor Claudius, and thus helped to precipitate the Roman invasion of Britain. Meantime his kingdom, which he extended into Kent, flourished, and the vine leaf on his coins emphasized the trade links with the Roman world, as did the ear of corn on Catuvellaunian coins north of the Thames.

Coin portraits of
Tincommius (*above*), king of
the south British Atrebates
(*c.* 25 BC–AD 5), and his
brother Verica. The
Romanizing tendency of these
chieftains is reflected in the
classical details of the
portraits, which may
nevertheless be fair likenesses.

Right, Tasciovanus, king of the Catuvellauni (*c.* 20 BC–AD 5), the Hertfordshire-based people who fiercely opposed Caesar. The title *rigonus* rather than the Roman *rex* on another Tasciovanus coin (*below*) attests to his conscious Celticism.

The Catuvellauni's tribal capital had been removed from Wheathampstead to Prae Wood, overlooking the future site of Verulamium (St Albans), probably by Cassivellaunus, who continued to rule (and presumably to pay tribute to Rome) until he was succeeded about 20 BC by Tasciovanus, his son or grandson. The latter appears to have attacked Camulodunum (Colchester), the capital of the Trinovantes (at any rate some rare coins of Tasciovanus bear this mint mark). Possibly he was encouraged to risk this act of aggression by news of a Roman military setback on the Rhine in 17 BC. However, Augustus' visit to Gaul in the following year may well have suggested the wisdom of a hasty retreat. Nevertheless Tasciovanus expanded his kingdom successfully northwards into Northamptonshire, and possibly into part of Kent, where some of his coins proclaim him as RIGONUS, advertising his preference for a Celtic title in place of the Roman REX. Camulodunum meanwhile was occupied for a short while by Dubnovellaunus, a Kentish ruler who had been driven out by Eppillus (*c.* AD 17?), but, like Tincommius, he was forced to flee to Augustus. The emperor regarded the arrival of these two British chiefs as sufficiently noteworthy to be recorded in the official account of his reign, the *Res Gestae*.

Dubnovellaunus had been driven from Camulodunum by Tasciovanus' son, Cunobelinus (Shakespeare's Cymbeline), who now absorbed the Trinovantes into his enlarged Catuvellaunian empire. Augustus made no

move: if Cunobelinus' aggression took place about AD 9, the emperor had much more serious matters preying on his mind, namely the defeat of his commander Varus and three legions in the Teutoburgian forest in western Germany. In fact Cunobelinus may even have won Augustus' favour, since he was probably one of the British rulers (Verica being another) who according to Strabo were allowed to send embassies to Rome and set up offerings on the Capitol. These were probably the rulers, then, who in Strabo's words 'made Britain almost a Roman country', a phrase which could have a political sting as well as an economic meaning. It was Roman policy to control areas beyond the frontiers of empire by means of client kings. Nor did Cunobelinus fare any worse under Tiberius, who allowed him to expand into Kent and took no action when Tasciovanus' other son, Epaticcus, occupied Verica's capital at Silchester (Calleva) about AD 25. When Cunobelinus died in AD 40 or 41, Verica shortly afterwards lost the rest of his kingdom and fled to Claudius.

Cunobelinus had become the most powerful British king of his time, and his realm had expanded and prospered. The capital at Colchester (Camulodunum, 'the fort of Camulos', the war god) was strongly guarded by a complicated system of dikes as well as by two river valleys. It also provided easy access to the coast and thus promoted an increasing volume of

Cunobelinus (Cymbeline) ruled the powerful Catuvellauni c. AD 5–40, greatly expanding the tribe's territory while introducing Roman products and practices at his new court of Colchester (Camulodunum).

31

overseas trade, as attested by the survival of numerous pottery cups and plates, and vessels which had brought wine and oil from the Continent and Italy itself (e.g. Arretine ware). Imported goods also included luxuries such as bracelets, necklaces, amber and glassware (so Strabo records), but they had to be paid for by exports which he specifies as wheat, cattle, gold, silver, iron, hides, slaves and hunting dogs. To this list pearls should perhaps be added, while tin is noticeably absent: Rome was now receiving the product of northwest Spain at the expense of the Cornish miners. Slavery was, of course, widespread in the Graeco-Roman world, and its existence in Britain is grimly attested by the discovery of chains for slave gangs in several places, including the hillfort at Bigbury.

But exaggeration must be avoided. Despite the luxury imports, which traders perhaps brought up the river Colne, Camulodunum remained a Celtic settlement. It had not yet become a Graeco-Roman city. The king and his followers might enjoy some of the products of Mediterranean civilization, but life for the ordinary man must have remained fairly primitive if not sordid. The town had a mint and a sacred area, but the buildings comprised groups of timber and wattle and daub huts, not unlike those found at Little Woodbury, protected by the extensive system of dikes. Yet in themselves these fortifications proclaimed the power of rulers who could organize and control so large a building operation. For the majority of Britons agriculture, of course, remained the basic way of life, but gradually the mineral wealth of the island, apart from tin, was being tapped and trade developed. Cunobelinus' rich kingdom remained essentially British in style, but since the wealthier class was beginning to supplement the fine products of Celtic metalware with foreign luxuries, Rome and Britain were clearly coming closer together.

THE OTHER TRIBES

The two main Belgic kingdoms, whose fortunes we have briefly followed, were not, of course, the only important tribal areas. Next to them lay the tribes which had absorbed to a greater or lesser degree something of Belgic culture, e.g. pottery and coinage; here a Belgic aristocracy appears to have imposed itself upon the indigenous Iron Age population. Beyond these, in the north and west, largely in the highland zone, were other tribal groups as yet untouched by Belgic influence. The former group included the Iceni, Coritani, Dobunni and Durotriges. The Iceni lived north of Cunobelinus' kingdom in Norfolk and part of Suffolk. Their coins, gold as well as silver, tell us the names of some of their kings, while the treasure found at Snettisham shows that their nobles were enjoying the benefits of a late Iron Age culture which was increasingly influenced by the more Romanized culture at Camulodunum. North of the Iceni, in Lincolnshire, Leicestershire and Nottinghamshire, dwelt the Coritani who were probably at loggerheads with the Catuvellauni, with the result that they were more pro-Roman.

The Dobunni, farther west in Gloucestershire and adjacent areas, were controlled by a Belgic aristocracy, while their basic Iron Age population was

Coin of the Iceni, the Norfolk tribe from which the warrior queen Boudicca came.

very advanced, as shown for instance by the Birdlip mirror. Here again their coins, which were less Romanized than those of the Atrebates, record the names of some of their rulers, who expanded their influence beyond their original nucleus; the centre at Corinium (Cirencester) later became one of the largest towns in Roman Britain. Finds made at one of their chief settlements at Bagendon suggest trade (and peaceful relations?) with the Catuvellauni. The last member of this group, the Durotriges, lived in Dorset and surrounding districts. They suffered a decline in their earlier lively cross-Channel trade with Brittany (Armorica) after Caesar's invasion, but like the Dobunni, they turned to trade with the Catuvellauni. Their hillforts included the massive Maiden Castle near Dorchester, whose fortifications were strengthened with a wooden palisade, Hod Hill, Hambledon and one on Hengistbury Head. Since many of their hillforts continued to be used, the Durotriges perhaps suffered from internal tribal struggles longer than some of their neighbours. Similar conditions are found among the smaller tribes around Salisbury Plain. Later the Romans welded some of these into a canton of Belgae with its capital at Winchester, and including part of what had been the territory of the Dobunni and the Atrebates.

Peripheral to these partly Belgicized areas were the tribes of the Cornish peninsula, Wales and the north, who were still untouched by Belgic influences. Cornwall, Devon and parts of Somerset comprised the land of the

Hod Hill, Dorset, a hillfort stronghold of the Durotriges, captured by the Romans in AD 44.

Dumnonii. Their hillforts in the extreme west differ from those in Wessex, being either cliff castles (like those in southern Brittany) or ringworks which may find their prototypes in Spain. The Dumnonii, therefore, represent the Iron Age immigrants who came to Cornwall partly in quest of tin, and then spread up the Bristol Channel into Somerset, where they established the lake villages of Glastonbury and Meare. Others pushed on up the Severn into South Wales. Numerous finds at these villages reveal the skilled work-manship of a people whom the pioneer explorer Pytheas had encountered, as we have seen, in their tin commerce from St Michael's Mount, and whom he described as 'friendly to strangers'. They appear to have suffered some aggression and penetration from the Durotriges on their eastern flank.

In Wales the less fertile and wilder countryside forced upon its inhabitants a more rugged and pastoral life. The Silures in southwest Wales, who according to Tacitus were dark in complexion and curly-haired (which suggested to him an Iberian origin), and the Delmatae of the somewhat more fertile Dyfed area, built earthworks similar to those in Cornwall. The Ordovices of the mountain fastnesses of North Wales could supplement their hilly pasturage with the agricultural produce of the Llyn peninsula and of Anglesey (Mona), where the headquarters of the Druids was based. The Deceangli of Clwyd (Flint and Denbigh) on the Welsh Marches, who have left their name enshrined at Deganwy, had a rich store of copper and lead. To their east in Salop, Cheshire and Staffordshire lived the Cornovii, whose centre may have been the Wrekin.

A great part of northern Britain was occupied by the Brigantes, who according to Tacitus were the largest tribe in Britain. They 'stretched from sea to sea', according to Ptolemy, and reached from southern Lancashire as far north as, or beyond, the line taken later by Hadrian's Wall. The East Riding of Yorkshire, however, was held by the Parisi, an Iron Age people who had been joined by other invaders from the Seine-Marne district, as shown by their custom of chariot burials, and by the name which they shared with their mother tribe in Gaul. The Brigantes, however, a much more backward people whose economy was basically pastoral, well fit Caesar's description: 'The people of the interior for the most part do not grow corn but live on milk and meat and dress in skins.' They were thus still living largely in Bronze Age conditions, although a few hillforts and chariot burials represent Iron Age developments, as shown by the metalwork found in a hoard at the vast hillfort of Stanwick. With the population separated into groups by wild moorland, political cohesion was slow to emerge but had probably been achieved by the time of the Claudian invasion of Britain (AD 43).

In Lowland Scotland, south of the Forth–Clyde isthmus, lived four tribes (the Novantae, the Damnonii, the Selgovae and the Votadini). Their hillforts were more numerous than those of the Brigantes, and their land more adapted to agriculture. Some more advanced aspects of their culture were probably brought by warriors driven out of southern Britain, who presumably arrived by sea, since their passage cannot be traced by land through Brigantian territory. North of the Forth–Clyde line in Caledonia, 'stern and wild', dwelt eleven tribes whose names are preserved by Ptolemy. In the extreme north the pattern of settlement assumed a different aspect, with fortified homesteads (brochs) emphasizing the importance of family units in defence. Even at the beginning of the third century AD, when they had to face attack by Septimius Severus, these Caledonian tribes remained wild. According to the historian Dio Cassius they lived in tents, naked and unshod, and possessed their women in common. They lived off their flocks, wild game and certain fruits, but neglected the abundant supplies of fish available. They fought in chariots and had small fast horses, while their foot soldiers, described as swift in running and firm in standing their ground, were each armed with a shield, a dagger and a short spear with a bronze apple attached to the shaft, designed to clash and frighten. They could survive half-submerged in swamps for many days, and could live in the forests on bark and roots. Another historian, Herodian, adds that the reason why they were practically naked was that they did not want to hide the pictures tattooed on their bodies. They also decorated their waists and necks with iron, which they valued as other barbarians valued gold.

From all this it may be seen that when Claudius' army landed in southern Britain the island presented a mosaic of tribal areas, enjoying very varied levels of culture.

Stages of the Roman conquest.

3

Conquest, occupation and Romanization

After one hundred years of freedom from external aggression (though not from internal dynastic fighting) many a Briton in the spring of AD 40 must have learnt with amazement and alarm that a Roman army was poised on the other shore of the English Channel, about to pounce. The emperor Gaius (Caligula) was on the point of launching an invasion. However, he then suddenly called it off, using as an excuse the fact that Cunobelinus' exiled son Adminius had fled to him and promised submission – Britain was as good as conquered, and so no expedition was needed! Gaius' real reasons remain obscure, but his troops were reluctant, if not mutinous, and he may have realized that if he went so far afield his authority in Rome might be at risk. Or he may simply have inconsequentially changed his mind, which was to some extent unbalanced, as may be gathered from the anecdote that on the Channel shore he ordered his troops to pick up seashells (*musculi*), the 'spoils of the Ocean' which had now been conquered! However he left behind one memorial: a new lighthouse at Boulogne.

If the Britons breathed a sigh of relief they were too sanguine, for within a short time Gaius had been murdered and Claudius, his successor, determined to conquer Britain, one of his reasons being that he felt Rome's military prestige had been unworthily compromised by Gaius' mad escapade. He was reinforced in his decision by many considerations. The situation in Britain was changing. On Cunobelinus' death his kingdom was divided between Togodumnus and Caratacus, who proceeded to attack the Dobunni and then robbed Verica of his remaining hold on the Atrebatic kingdom. Verica reacted by following Adminius' example of appealing to the Roman emperor; even if he had not technically been recognized as a client king of Rome (despite the REX on his coins), at least Rome might feel that she owed him some help. Again, Claudius had not shared in any military campaigns, and his armies would like to see him extending the empire and reviving Rome's martial traditions. He may also have wished to stamp out Druidism at its source in Britain, since Augustus and Tiberius had both checked it in Gaul. Another attraction was the wealth of Britain, which could now be assessed better than in Julius Caesar's day. In any case, the thought of annexing Britain had been 'in the air' in the time of Augustus. Claudius would now carry it out.

In AD 43 four legions were mustered: II Augusta, XIV Gemina, XX Valeria Victrix and IX Hispana. They were commanded by Aulus Plautius and accompanied by auxiliary troops, making in all a force of some 40,000 men. After a show of reluctance they eventually set sail in three

The emperor Claudius, who initiated the Roman invasion of AD 43. This contemporary head, found in the river Alde, Suffolk, may have been left there by Boudicca's troops following the destruction of Colchester.

divisions. The main force landed in the safety of the harbour of Richborough (Rutupiae), where traces of their beach-head defences still survive. After some skirmishes in east Kent came the encouraging news that some of the Dobunni much further west were offering to surrender. But the Romans had yet to cross the river Medway where the enemy were massed and here, perhaps near Rochester, came the decisive battle. The Roman auxiliaries managed to swim across in full equipment, and after a two-day struggle the Romans were victorious, helped greatly by the actions of Vespasian, commander of the Second Legion. The enemy retired to the Thames, which the auxiliaries again forded, and Togodumnus was killed in a minor skirmish. Plautius then halted the advance until Claudius could arrive from Italy and lead his troops in person to a final victory north of the Thames.

The emperor duly arrived, with a distinguished staff and some elephants with which to overawe the natives. He watched his troops storm Colchester, which he established as the capital for the new province of Britannia. He also received the submission of other tribes. Verica, if still alive, was probably restored to his kingdom, but he was soon succeeded by Cogidubnus as king of the Regni, with his capital at Chichester (Noviomagus) in Sussex. He was granted Roman citizenship (becoming Tiberius Claudius Cogidubnus), and with the title of *rex et legatus Augusti* became both local king and the emperor's deputy. His kingdom was probably enlarged as a result. In East Anglia too the Iceni submitted under their king (Prasutagus or his predecessor), and were accorded Roman friendship. Cartimandua, queen of the Brigantes, also gained Rome's favour, possibly as early as AD 43. With its borders now adequately protected by client kings, the new province could safely be left in the charge of its first governor, Plautius. Claudius, after sixteen days in Britain, returned to Rome where he celebrated a magnificent triumph – the first held by a reigning emperor for some 70 years. To emphasize his achievement he also named his son Britannicus.

In the Campus Martius the Senate and Roman People set up an arch in his honour with an inscription proclaiming that 'he subdued eleven kings of Britain without any reverse, and received their surrender, and was the first to bring barbarian nations beyond the Ocean under Roman sway'. No doubt the provinces of the empire were equally quick to honour him, and we have one example of a more private initiative of this kind from the Athletes' Guild at Pisidian Antioch. In his reply Claudius wrote (his rescript is preserved in a Greek papyrus): 'I received with pleasure the gold crown that you sent me on the occasion of my victory over the Britons, as a perpetual token of your loyalty to me.' But Claudius gave as well as received honours, and there are inscriptions recording military decorations made to serving soldiers: C. Gavius Silvanus, for instance, who was probably in the ranks of the Praetorian Guard, 'was granted neck-chains, armlets, medals and a gold crown in the British war by the emperor Claudius', and P. Anicius Maximus, camp prefect of the II Legio Augusta in Britain, was honoured with a mural crown and a silver spear *ob bellum Britannicum*.

Although Caratacus had escaped and was still at large in Wales, the Romans decided to secure the lowlands before hunting him down. Plautius

An *aureus* (sovereign) of Claudius, AD 51–2, celebrating his victory over the Britons.

Skeletons found at Maiden Castle, Dorset, scene of a savage battle between the native Durotriges and the Roman invading forces under Vespasian.

immediately planned a synchronized three-pronged advance. From the base at Colchester Legio IX, the right wing, struck northwards towards Lincoln (Lindum), and some of the marching camps and forts that marked its advance have been identified. Legio XIV made its way through the Midlands along the line of Watling Street towards Leicester (Ratae). Meanwhile the future emperor Vespasian led Legio II westwards, reduced the Isle of Wight (Vectis) – store buildings suggest that Fishbourne near Chichester was his base for this operation – and then pressed on westwards. He reduced over twenty *oppida* and 'two powerful tribes', the Durotriges and the Dumnonii. Dramatic evidence survives of the grimness of these struggles and the storming of the great hillforts such as Maiden Castle, where buried skeletons reveal sword cuts and even an iron arrowhead lodged in the victim's spine. The Romans drove the defenders from the massive earthwork ramparts with shots from their artillery (*ballistae*), and then set fire to the wooden gates. *Ballista* missiles mark the capture of another hillfort, at Hod Hill near Blandford in Dorset, where the Romans then established a camp of their own for legionary detachments and cavalry. The advance continued at least as far as Exeter, but the Roman fort in Cornwall at Nanstallon, near Bodmin, appears to be Neronian rather than Claudian. Then, when the Severn and the Wash had been reached, Plautius called a temporary halt and created a deep military frontier zone based on the Fosse Way from Exeter to Lincoln (continuing along Ermine Street to the Humber). Here legionary detachments (*vexillationes*) were permanently quartered near the front line, together with a back-up of auxiliary forts where needed. Having thus provided the new province of southeast Britain with this protective shield, Aulus Plautius retired with honour from his command in AD 47.

His successor, P. Ostorius Scapula (47–52), faced with disturbances among the Silures in South Wales and a restless Brigantia in northern England, became convinced that the protection of the lowlands demanded further advance. As a preliminary he decided to disarm all tribes south of the Fosse Way, which brought a hostile reaction from the Iceni; perhaps the creation of a large 27-acre fortress at Longthorpe near Peterborough, excavated in 1967–71, was a counter-measure. He then planned to advance into the gap between the Severn and Trent, pushing forward the Midland troops, though perhaps not yet as far as Wroxeter (Viroconium or Uriconium): a very large camp of nearly 50 acres was revealed by the drought of the summer of 1976 near Chirk in Salop, controlling the approaches to the vale of Llangollen, and this fort may well have formed Ostorius' base when he advanced into the Cheshire gap against the Deceangli. At any rate, after subduing the Deceangli and helping Cartimandua to quieten the Brigantes, he turned to the Silures, establishing a legionary base at Kingsholme near Gloucester (Glevum), and building a network of forts and military roads.

Caratacus, who had taken refuge among the Silures, had no intention of being caught like a rat in a trap and managed to escape to the Ordovices in the yet wilder parts of North Wales. However, he was eventually met and defeated in a pitched battle (possibly near Caersws), from which he escaped to Cartimandua. The Brigantian queen handed him over to the Romans (AD 51), but he was pardoned by Claudius, who was impressed by his defiant courage and allowed him to live in Rome in honourable confinement.

By these means Ostorius made the frontiers of the new province more secure. He also began to promote its 'Romanization', establishing a colony of veterans at Colchester (Camulodunum), where the town was being developed on Roman lines as a worthy provincial capital with a temple of Claudius as the centre of the imperial cult (see p. 155). This was the first colony in the province. It is uncertain whether Claudius gave a municipal charter (granting Latin status) to St Albans (Verulamium) which was founded about the same time as Colchester. Britain's second governor died suddenly, worn out by his efforts, but he had proved no less efficient than its first.

The next two governors checked the Silures (a fortress was established at Usk *c.* AD 55), and reinstated Cartimandua, who had been deposed by her consort Venutius, while in the south towns such as London, Canterbury and Silchester began to expand under Roman influence. The next push forward was made by Suetonius Paulinus, who ended resistance in South Wales, overran the Deceangli, and launched an attack on Anglesey (Mona), which was a supply base and a refuge for Rome's enemies in Britain as well as a centre of the Druids. The far-flung influence of this religious order is dramatically illustrated by the discovery of a hoard of offerings at Llyn Cerrig Bach in Anglesey. These objects, which had been thrown into a lake at this time either by the threatened Druids themselves (to save them, or to appease their gods) or else by the avenging Romans, show in the variety of their origins from how wide an area in Britain the Druids could claim offerings. Although the Roman troops wavered at first in face of the defenders backed by priests with supposed supernatural powers, Suetonius forced the Menai Strait, and set about felling the sacred groves and settling the island. But while thus engaged he heard that Boudicca and the Iceni had revolted in his rear.

The Iceni had long been suffering from the exactions of Roman tax-collectors and Roman money-lenders, who included the philosopher Seneca. In 60 (rather than in 61) their king Prasutagus died. Since he had no son, Nero who was now emperor appears to have decided to absorb the area into the Roman province, rather than to recognize Prasutagus' widow Boudicca (Boadicea). When Roman officials seized land for the emperor which Claudius had granted to tribal nobles, and when finally Boudicca was scourged and her daughters were violated, the whole tribe rose in revolt. The historian Dio Cassius has described the scene as the queen harangued her warriors, grasping a spear in her hand: 'In stature she was very tall, in appearance most terrifying, her glance was fierce, her voice harsh; a great mass of the tawniest hair fell to her hips; around her neck was a large golden torc; she wore, as usual, a tunic of various colours over which a thick mantle was fastened with a brooch.' The Iceni were joined in revolt by the Trinovantes, who were indignant at the confiscation of some of their land for the Roman colonists at Colchester, and also at the cost of the upkeep of Claudius' temple and cult, the hated 'arx aeternae dominationis' which symbolized their subjection.

The rebels moved first against Colchester, which was unwalled, while the nearest Roman legions were over 100 miles away. In two days the town was overwhelmed and all the Roman survivors, men, women and children, were butchered. Part of the Ninth Legion, hastily summoned from Lincoln, was defeated with overwhelming loss, though its commander Petilius Cerialis and the cavalry escaped. Meanwhile Suetonius took the bold decision to hasten from Wales to London ahead of his main troops. But when neither his own legions arrived nor the Second Legion which he had summoned from the southwest (Exeter?), he had to abandon both London and St Albans to Boudicca's fury. Seventy thousand people were said to have perished in the sack of the three towns, and burnt debris and skeletons found at Spitalfields bear witness to the onslaught. Suetonius withdrew along Watling Street, and then stood and fought, although heavily outnumbered and deserted by the Second Legion, whose commander had disobeyed his order to come to the rescue.

On ground of his own choosing, perhaps at a site near Lichfield or at Mancetter north of Coventry, his disciplined forces utterly routed Boudicca, who took poison. Supported by some reinforcements from the Rhineland, Suetonius then began to carry out savage reprisals, but the new financial officer, Julius Classicianus, recoiled from such violence. Since these

Tombstone of Julius Classicianus, the procurator (financial officer) who intervened to prevent savage retaliation after Boudicca's rebellion.

procurators had some authority independent of the governor, Classicianus sent in a report to Nero urging a more lenient policy. His appeal was upheld, and Suetonius was superseded. His successors, C. Petronius Turpilianus and M. Trebellius Maximus, pursued a more conciliatory line, and Britain settled down to a period of peace and growth. The west was guarded by a new fortress at Gloucester itself, and an even larger base of 51 acres at Usk. These quieter days were not disrupted too seriously by the troubles during the Year of the Four Emperors (AD 69) when the army groups in different parts of the empire put forward their own commanders as claimants to the throne. Classicianus died in Britain, and his tombstone still survives in London, which seems to have recovered remarkably quickly from its sack and had become the centre both of the administrative system of the province and of its road system (see p. 55).

ADVANCE UNDER THE FLAVIAN EMPERORS

Vespasian and his sons Titus and Domitian (the Flavian dynasty, AD 69–96) restored stability and security to the Roman empire, but in Britain

A running boar was one of the emblems of Legio XX Valeria Victrix, which played a key role in the conquest and settlement of Britain.

they planned further conquest. The alliance with Brigantia in the north had already broken down, and Venutius, husband of the Brigantian queen Cartimandua, had long been fomenting an anti-Roman faction. When Cartimandua divorced him he openly attacked her, driving her to appeal to Rome for help. She herself was rescued by the Roman governor, Vettius Bolanus, but Venutius held on to the kingdom. Vettius' successor, Q. Petilius Cerialis, who arrived in AD 71, was sent out by Vespasian to take action against Rome's enemies beyond the frontiers of the province. He brought with him a new legion, II Adiutrix, to replace XIV Gemina which had been withdrawn in 67 by Nero for service in the East.

Advancing from Lincoln, where earlier he had served under Paulinus, Cerialis moved his legionary headquarters up to York (Eboracum), strategically a well-chosen spot. Helped by a pincer movement led by the famous Agricola, then legate of Legio XX, from Wroxeter (Viroconium) and the west, he defeated Venutius, probably at the great hillfort at Stanwick.

His successor, Sextus Iulius Frontinus (74–8), a skilled engineer and an expert on aqueducts, resumed the advance into Wales. He moved Legio II to a new fortress at Caerleon (Isca Silurum) near the mouth of the Usk, and built some forts to guard the south coast of Wales, i.e. at Cardiff, Neath and Carmarthen. After defeating the Silures in battle, he destroyed their stronghold at Llanmelin Wood and provided them with a new town at Caerwent (Venta Silurum), where they would be under the eye of the legion stationed at Caerleon. Frontinus also built many roads and forts further north, for instance around Brecon (Y Gaer and Castell Collen), and in the Upper Severn valley (Caersws), and started constructing a fortress at Chester (Deva). He also attacked the Ordovices, in whose territory he planted some garrisons. Although he did not complete their conquest, he laid down a network of roads and forts which provided the pattern for the subjugation of the whole of Wales.

Frontinus was followed as governor by Cn. Iulius Agricola, who had already served in Britain. Since he was familiar with North Wales he immediately made that his first objective, defeating the Ordovices and overrunning Anglesey. He established forts at Caernarvon (Segontium) and at Caerhun in the Conway valley, if his predecessor had not already done so. In AD 79 he overawed Brigantia, sending in his troops in two parallel columns, one from York in the east, the other from Chester in the west, which thus isolated the Lake District. They reached the Tyne–Solway line, where later Hadrian's Wall was to run. In the next year they advanced in two columns, one on each side of the central spine of hills, and so conquered the Lowlands of Scotland, reaching the Tanaus (probably the Tay). In 81 Agricola consolidated his advance, and built some forts which very roughly followed the line of the later Antonine Wall. In 82 he turned successfully against the Novantae in southwest Scotland, and a recently discovered fort, south of Annan in Dumfriesshire, could have provided the beach-head for a seaborne landing. He had some knowledge of Ireland, having received an exiled Irish prince, and is alleged to have said that the island could be conquered by a single legion; but he made no move to put his prediction to the test.

Domitian, who had now become emperor, was prepared to order further advance and the conquest of the whole of Scotland, not merely the Lowlands. So in 83 Agricola continued the expansion northwards, although now he was forced to march in one column only up along the eastern plains. His supply lines were dangerously extended, but he blocked the approaches from the Highlands on the left flank with forts at the exits of the glens, while his fleet could be used to help bring up supplies. The most westerly of this chain of some eight forts which blocked the southern edge of the Highland massif was discovered in 1977 on Drumquhassie Ridge, south of Loch Lomond. After beating off an attack, the Roman army reached the neighbourhood of Aberdeen, and a legionary fortress was started at Inchtuthil. In 84 the Caledonians, who formed a confederacy under Calgacus and allegedly raised some 30,000 men, awaited the Romans at Mons Graupius (perhaps near Inverness), where they foolishly risked a pitched battle. The brunt of their attack fell on the Roman auxiliaries rather than the legions, but Rome's victory was decisive, and Scotland was effectively conquered. Agricola's task was now completed. He sent his fleet to explore the Orkneys and sail round the north of Britain to establish that it *was* an island; he himself returned to Rome after a long governorship of seven years.

The conquest of northern Scotland had presumably been ordered by Domitian, but he was soon forced to change this policy. In AD 83 he had to face unexpected Dacian attacks from Romania over the Danube. To meet this very serious threat more troops were urgently needed, and so Legio II was rushed from Chester to Moesia (Serbia), while Legio XX had to come down from Inchtuthil to Chester. But if in the future only three legions could be spared to form the standing garrison of Britain, it was evidently necessary for Domitian to undertake a reappraisal of the size of the province. He decided to abandon the legionary fortress at Inchtuthil, which in fact had not been completed, and with it all plans for occupation north of the isthmus. This abandonment of northern Scotland was not carried out in a hurry, but it occasioned Tacitus' bitter remark that 'the conquest of Britain was completed and immediately let go' (*perdomita Britannia et statim omissa*). Tacitus, who was Agricola's son-in-law, might regard this policy as a negation of all Agricola's work and attribute it to Domitian's jealousy, but it was apparently inevitable unless further troops (legionaries and still more auxiliaries) could be spared for this distant province at a time when the manpower of the empire was fully stretched. Agricola could perhaps more justly complain that the emperor did not entrust him with any further major command, but Britain, including the Lowlands of Scotland, was held by three legions stationed on the edges of the English plain (II Augusta at Caerleon, XX Valeria Victrix at Chester, and IX Hispana at York), while auxiliary cohorts were distributed over Wales and garrisoned northern Britain as far as the Forth and the Clyde.

The conquest of the province was celebrated by the construction of a great monument at Richborough, one of the main ports of entry to the island, where it would impress all visitors. It consisted of a four-way triumphal arch, nearly 90 feet high, magnificently adorned with bronze statues and marble brought from Italy. All that survives is a cross-shaped base for the marble-paved passageway between the arches (see p. 66), for it was destroyed later when the fort of the Saxon Shore was set up. But it was definitely built in the Flavian period, and may well have been Agricola's final trumpet blast as he left the island.

AGRICOLA AND THE ROMANIZATION OF BRITAIN

Since Agricola is the one governor of Britain about whom we know any details, we have an opportunity to see briefly what sort of man he was. This is possible thanks to the panegyrical biography composed by his son-in-law, the historian Tacitus, although allowance must be made for some bias by the biographer on both family and political grounds. Gnaeus Iulius Agricola was a provincial, born in AD 40 at Forum Iulii (Fréjus) in Romanized southern Gaul. His grandfathers were procurators of equestrian rank; his father, a Roman senator and praetor, incurred Caligula's displeasure and was executed. His mother, a cultured lady, sent him to be educated at the Graeco-

Roman city of Marseilles, where he studied rhetoric and philosophy. He started his official career as military tribune in Britain in years of peace and war under the governor Suetonius Paulinus (58–61). After a quaestorship in Asia, where he refused to connive at the activities of an unscrupulous proconsul, he held offices in Rome and then returned to Britain as a legionary commander. Enrolment in the patriciate by Vespasian and a governorship of Aquitania (southwest France) were followed by a consulship (77). Then came the governorship of Britain, which he held for the unprecedented term of seven years. By nature he was straightforward, honest and moderate; he did not spare himself and showed concern for the feelings of the native population (*animorum provinciae prudens*). 'Beginning with himself and his staff, he put his own house in order, a task not less difficult for most governors than the government of a province.' He showed personal impartiality to all alike, and was lenient towards small offences but severe towards major ones. He repressed abuses, especially in the tax-collecting system. In conclusion Tacitus writes: 'You would readily have believed him to be a good man, and gladly to be a great one' (*bonum virum facile crederes, magnum libenter*).

His military abilities were very considerable, but in addition to victory in battle his achievements included building over 1,300 miles of roads and at least 60 forts, while archaeology corroborates the judgment of contemporary experts, recorded by Tacitus, regarding his skill in the choice of camp sites. But this represented only one side of his work in Britain, which was actively complemented by a policy of encouraging the spread of Roman civilization. The famous passage in which Tacitus describes this deserves quotation:

In order that a people, hitherto scattered and uncivilized and therefore ready for war, might become accustomed to peace and ease, Agricola encouraged individuals and helped communities to build temples, fora and houses. . . . Further, he trained the sons of the chiefs in the liberal arts and expressed a preference for British natural ability over the trained abilities of the Gauls. The result was that the people who used to reject the Latin language, began to aspire to rhetoric. Further, the wearing of our national dress came to be esteemed and the toga came into fashion. And so, little by little, the Britons were seduced into alluring vices: arcades, baths and sumptuous banquets. In their simplicity they called such novelties 'civilization', when in reality they were part of their enslavement.

The aspects of Romanization mentioned by Tacitus will be discussed in detail later on, but here we may consider briefly his main points, and see how far 'the policy of conquest by assimilation' (I. A. Richmond) had advanced at this stage of the Roman occupation. The most striking change, which was to transfigure the face of Britain, was urbanization. Large or small, towns were an essential element in Roman Britain, and to a very considerable extent the deliberate gift of the Romans. Ancient Mediterranean civilization was based on the life of the city (even though its economic roots were still essentially agricultural), and for the Greeks and Romans the city embodied the best life. When Pericles urged the Athenians to become 'lovers of their city' he was thinking of a community based on a physical city.

The Romans, too, used the city as an instrument for the civilizing of Italy and the less developed parts of their empire. When in Britain they moved

native tribes from their hill fortresses to towns on lower ground, as at Prae Wood to Verulamium, or from Llanmelin to Caerwent, they were continuing a policy which they had followed in Italy, Spain and Gaul. They were forcing a new way of life on Celtic peoples to whom it was at first alien. Before the Romans arrived, there were no real towns in Britain. The native settlements were largely mere conglomerations of huts protected by widespread dikes, as at Prae Wood or Wheathampstead, or more compact hillforts providing centres to which the surrounding population could flee in time of danger. The life within these settlements was probably fairly primitive. The fact that the Romans not only imposed organized town life on the Britons, but actually persuaded them to adopt and develop this new way of life for themselves throughout a greater part of the island, was no mean achievement – by both parties.

After conquering and annexing foreign territory the Romans had to face the problem of local administration. They could impose a general over-all control, but they needed the cooperation of the natives for the running of day-to-day affairs. This involved allowing them as much self-government as was compatible with orderly administration. Roman policy was always to accept and adapt whatever units they found in the provinces, be they cities or tribes. They preferred working through cities, which of course had already existed for centuries in the Greek and eastern parts of their empire. In the more backward western part, in Gaul, Spain and Britain, they acted through the existing tribal units and at the same time promoted the development of towns as quickly as they could in those areas where this was feasible. The local tribal centres of the cantons (*civitates*) were encouraged to develop into Roman towns (*vici*), while at the same time the inhabitants remained citizens of their tribe and not of the town: thus the inhabitants of Wroxeter (Viroconium) were *cives Cornovii*, not *Viroconienses*.

These emergent native cantonal centres found their model in the Roman towns known as *coloniae* (settlements of Roman citizens), which in Britain were very few in number. One of these, consisting of discharged legionaries and their families, was established alongside the native settlement at Colchester as early as AD 49, but it was not until near the end of the first century that two others followed, at Lincoln and Gloucester. A *municipium*, on the other hand, was an upgraded existing town which received a grant of either Roman or (the more limited) Latin rights. In the former case the inhabitants became Roman citizens, in the latter citizenship was initially granted only to the town magistrates, though later this was extended to the whole town council. Verulamium (St Albans) was made a *municipium*, probably with Latin rights, possibly under Claudius but more probably under Vespasian. Though evidence is lacking, in view of its importance London may well also have been made a *municipium* about AD 100.

But *municipia* and *coloniae*, whose internal administration is discussed later (p. 89), could not be created in large numbers, while native settlements could not be transformed into Roman towns overnight. The process was gradual and closely intermeshed with the pace of Roman conquest and occupation. Official Roman policy encouraged the movement, but as tribal areas were released from military control, the Romans did not impose any rigid plan, so

Opposite, the Romanization of Britain: two reconstructions from Cirencester (Corinium). *Above*, a dining-room (*triclinium*) with replicas of Roman furniture and hangings set out on a mosaic floor. *Below*, a kitchen with raised stone hearth, amphorae for imported wine and oil, various utensils, and an iron chain pothanger.

these native *civitas* tribal centres were allowed some variety in development. The precise point at which *civitates* emerged as such has been much debated, namely whether this occurred before or only after Roman military occupation had been completely withdrawn from an area. But whether the governor relaxed his grip gradually or more abruptly, the local tribal aristocracy assumed the role of local magistrates and councillors (*decuriones*), and began to exercise increasing independence in local administration, though in the last resort they were still subject to the governor's will. Moreover, these centres were gradually enhanced, not least under Agricola, with fora, basilicas and other buildings which administrative and social needs required.

The transition from tribe to *civitas* was in a sense cushioned by Rome's early establishment of client kingdoms, where the continuing authority of the native ruler as Rome's friend was recognized – as long as he remained loyal. This was a long-established aspect of Roman foreign policy. In the period of conquest three such areas were recognized by Rome: the Atrebates under Cogidubnus in the south, who were actually within the Roman province, the Iceni under Prasutagus, who were outside the province until Ostorius Scapula extended it to include them, and thus provoked the Boudiccan revolt, and the Brigantes under Cartimandua beyond the province. These arrangements lasted only for limited periods, namely until the revolt of Boudicca, the death of Cogidubnus (*c.* AD 80?) in the Flavian period, and Agricola's occupation of Brigantia. On their dissolution the Iceni (probably after a period of military rule) gained a *civitas* capital at Caistor-by-Norwich (Venta Icenorum) before the end of the century. The kingdom of Cogidubnus was split into three divisions: the *civitas Regnensium*, *civitas Atrebatum* and *civitas Belgarum*, with capitals respectively at Chichester (Noviomagus Regnensium), Silchester (Calleva Atrebatum), and Winchester (Venta Belgarum). The fate of the Brigantes is less clear, but ultimately, i.e. early in the second century, we find a *civitas* of the Brigantes at Aldborough (Isurium Brigantum) and a *civitas* of the Parisi at Brough-on-Humber (Petuaria).

The most outstanding of these three client rulers was Cogidubnus (*c.* AD 45–80), whose somewhat ambiguous position is proclaimed in an inscription from Chichester, recording the dedication of a temple:

To Neptune and Minerva this temple [is dedicated with prayers] for the welfare of the divine [i.e. imperial] house, by the authority of Tiberius Claudius Cogidubnus, king and imperial legate in Britain [*rex et legatus Augusti in Britannia*], by the guild of smiths and its members, at their own expense; Clemens, son of Prudentinus, presented the site.

Cogidubnus thus combined the roles of native chief and Roman official. The site of his early capital is uncertain, and Selsey, Fishbourne or Chichester are all possibilities. The palace at Fishbourne (p. 119) may well have provided him with a country retreat from a capital at Chichester. He encouraged Romanization throughout his realm to the best of his ability, as witness the temple to two Roman deities, even though the evidence for his building activity in Chichester may not be as strong as sometimes thought (despite the

NEPTVNO·ET·MINERVAE
TEMPLVM
PRO·SALVTE·DOMVS·DIVINAE
EX·AVCTORITATE·TI·CLAVD·
COGIDVBNI·REGIS·MAGN·BRIT·
COLLEGIVM·FABROR·ET·QVI·IN·EO
SVNT·D·S·D·DONANTE·AREAM
ENTE·PVDENTINI·FIL

dedication of a large building to the emperor Nero). His rule was obviously much the most successful of the three client kings.

Apart from the *civitates* which developed after the break-up of these client kingdoms, we know of many more. The earliest of all, before AD 50, were naturally those in the southeast. Capitals were established at Canterbury (Durovernum) for a new unit, the Cantiaci of Kent, at St Albans for the Catuvellauni, and at Chelmsford (Caesaromagus) for the Trinovantes. In the Flavian period at least five more *civitates* were established, in addition to the three that followed the death of Cogidubnus, the sites often being chosen in relation to pre-existing forts. These were at Exeter (Isca) for the Dumnonii, at Dorchester (Durnovaria) for the Durotriges, at Cirencester (Corinium) for the Dobunni, at Leicester (Ratae) for the Coritani, and (possibly a little later) at Wroxeter (Viroconium) for the Cornovii. Other *civitates* soon followed in the early second century, not only for the Brigantes and Parisi, as we have seen, but also at Caerwent (Venta Silurum) for the Silures and probably at Carmarthen (Moridunum) for the Demetae in South Wales. Some of the more advanced of these *civitas* capitals were possibly granted the higher status of municipal rights, while others were subdivided into smaller units, thus spreading self-government still further. The Durotriges, for instance, were later split between the original capital at Dorchester and a new capital at Ilchester.

To return to the beginning of this process of urbanization, we may now consider the early development of the three towns sacked by Boudicca. Colchester, the first and for a long time the only *colonia*, was built quickly by direct imperial orders for retired legionaries. Its relation to the previous settlements there and its early growth have been illuminated by recent excavations in the 1970s. When the Romans arrived in AD 43, the two areas of Belgic settlement at Colchester were allowed to continue, though a legionary fortress was immediately established only half a mile from the

From a Roman temple at Chichester, a dedicatory inscription reflects the Romanizing influence of Cogidubnus, an important British client king of the first century.

51

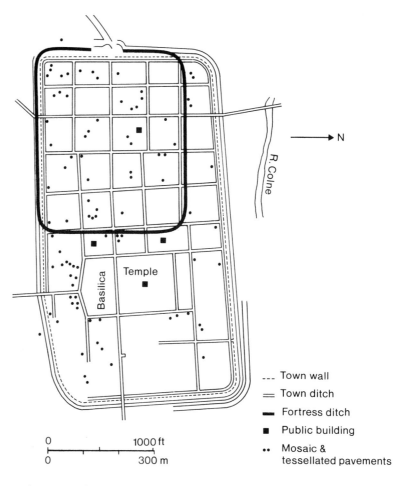

Early Roman Colchester.
The original legionary fortress
of AD 43 was soon
demilitarized to become part
of a much larger civilian
colonia for Roman citizens,
complete with a temple of the
imperial cult.

N

R. Colne

Basilica

Temple

--- Town wall
= Town ditch
— Fortress ditch
■ Public building
•• Mosaic &
tessellated pavements

0   1000 ft

0   300 m

settlement at Sheepen. A small fort was also placed (perhaps as early as 43)
near the other Belgic area two miles away, at Gosbecks Farm, where there
was a pre-Roman religious centre. Since the Romans apparently still allowed
congregations to gather there, they may have decided to keep a watchful eye
on these activities. The new excavations have shown where the original
legionary fortress was located, and how, after some six or seven years of
occupation, it was demilitarized and its defences destroyed in order to form
part of the much larger new *colonia* built over and to the east of it in *c.* AD 49.
The new eastern part of the town was dominated by the great temple of
Claudius and its surrounding sacred area (*temenos*).

Tacitus refers also to a senate house and theatre. Traces of these have not
yet been found, but excavation has revealed the massive foundations of the
temple, and has provided us with a glimpse of the timber-framed houses and
shops of the first veteran settlers under the burnt layers left by the Boudiccan
fire. The stock of one shop, consisting of Samian pottery and glass, has
survived amid the rubble. Another building contained wheat in one room,
30 bowls (*mortaria*) in another, and 80 flagons in a third. The native
inhabitants were included in the community; whether they lived within or

outside the town is a somewhat pointless question, since there was at this time no town wall to divide or unite the inhabitants. The Romans had assumed that the area was pacified and that no protective walls were needed, so that it became an open target for Boudicca's anger, and thereafter had to be completely rebuilt. By c. AD 75 the town had recovered to the extent that it was even beginning to expand, and its new public buildings included three which have recently been discovered: a Romano-Celtic temple, a square construction (perhaps a shrine), and a monumental arch which was later (early second to third century) incorporated into the new Balkerne Gate, at a time when the town was provided with a stone wall. Thus it was not long before a fine new town had sprung from the ashes.

St Albans on the other hand was thought until recently to have consisted of little more, before AD 61, than 'a straggle of shops and shacks' (A. L. F. Rivet). However, we now know that while the Catuvellauni in Prae Wood had been allowed to expand down to the river Ver, the town-planning of the new *civitas* capital, built on the opposite southern bank, had made a very good start with many streets going back to Claudian days. A block of timber-framed shops, for instance, a number of which were used for metalworking, can be dated to c. AD 49. The building technique of these shops repeats in some details that used by the Roman army, as exemplified at Valkenberg in Holland, the base from which the Claudian invasion had been launched. Thus in promoting urbanization the Romans clearly provided not only encouragement, but also training in the necessary skills of planning and construction, and this was given by the army. Most fora and baths (*thermae*) were based on military designs, resembling the *principia* and bath buildings of military camps. We do not know precisely how soon St Albans got all its public buildings, but a fine inscription tells us that Agricola dedicated a (new) forum in AD 79. The settlement area of about 119 acres appears to have been enclosed by a bank and ditch, but these were of little use against Boudicca's attack.

London, the third city to have been sacked by Boudicca, was at this time, according to Tacitus, 'thronged by a crowd of businessmen and merchants, though not distinguished by the title of a *colonia*'. Whatever activity there may have been on the site during the century between Caesar and Claudius, there is no evidence for permanent settlement in the area of the City of London before the Romans arrived in AD 43. The subsequent speedy development of the early town has been illuminated by recent excavations, especially those at the junction of Gracechurch Street and Fenchurch Street, where there are traces of a superficial occupation in c. 43, suggesting a military camp. This was followed by a period (c. 44–50) when roads and buildings were laid out on a regular plan, probably again of a military nature, with a military post and a bridge over the Thames being among the first requirements. The next ten years (c. 50–60) saw much replanning and development: timber-framed houses with clay floors and plastered walls, and even piped water along the main road. This growth was probably civilian rather than military, the one phase emerging from the other, as at Colchester, and reflects commercial exploitation of the site, both for trade in general and as a centre for supplies for the armies fighting in the north. Docks, too, must

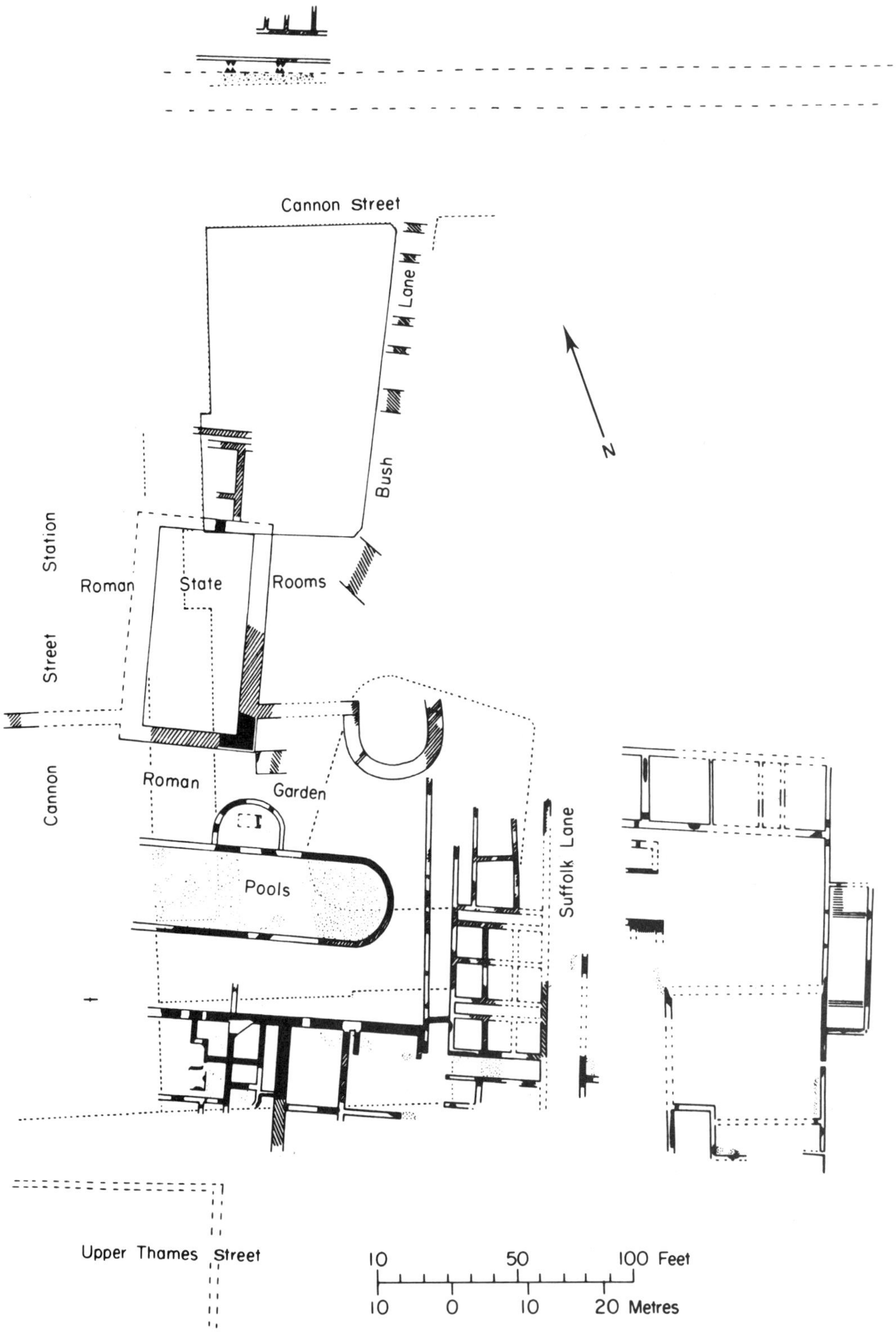

Cannon Street

Bush Lane

Station

Roman Street

Street

Cannon

Roman

State Rooms

Garden

Suffolk Lane

Pools

N

I

Upper Thames Street

10   50   100 Feet

10   0   10   20 Metres

have been developed. Thus London was quickly superseding Colchester, which had been the main trading centre. Its geographical position on the Thames may have been slightly more convenient than that of Colchester on the Colne, while its population was perhaps more diversified and energetic than the staid veterans of Colchester. Its importance was still further increased when the governor of the province moved his headquarters from Colchester to London, together with the financial offices, and its central position was demonstrated by the network of roads which began to spread across Britain, radiating from London, not Colchester. The administrative move was probably made early, before AD 60.

Then came the destruction by Boudicca and gradual recovery. Quite soon, starting in the decade 60–70, a massive structure covering some one and a half acres and including a central courtyard began to rise on the Fenchurch Street site. Named the 'proto-forum' by archaeologists, it was obviously used for administrative purposes and probably contained the *tabularium*, the treasury offices of the imperial procurator and his staff. Below are traces of a pre-Boudiccan building, suggesting that the transfer to London of Rome's financial headquarters may have been even earlier. Another complex of buildings from Cannon Street to the Thames front, containing a garden with fountains and an ornamental pool, was almost certainly the governor's palace. Its construction began *c.* AD 80, though his headquarters may, of course, have occupied the site earlier.

Two slightly later developments were a new forum and a fort. During the last decade of the century the 'proto-forum' site was redeveloped into the largest forum-basilica complex in Roman Britain. It measured some 550 feet square and covered approximately seven and a half acres, starting from Cornhill down to Lombard and Fenchurch Streets, with a monumental entrance on its southern side. It must have dominated the city. The second change was to provide the unwalled city with military protection; early in the second century a fort of some 11 acres was built in the Cripplegate area. Its garrison included men drawn from all the three legions who, as shown by their surviving tombstones, had been detached for duties at headquarters in London. So, too, was a certain Celsus, a member of a body of 30 *speculatores* seconded from their legions to serve mainly for judicial work on the governor's staff. One of those mentioned was a centurion, and since he is depicted on his tombstone as holding a scroll, he may well have been a *princeps praetorii*, the head of the governor's staff. The fort probably served for men such as these, as well as for the governor's guard (see plan p. 96).

The stimulus which Agricola and his predecessors provided for urbanization can be traced in some detail, thanks to the physical evidence of excavated buildings. Other economic developments cannot be followed in the same way, but the evidence of early lead-mining, about which something is known, shows that the Romans were far from slow in exploiting the deposits in the Mendip Hills, and suggests that they were probably equally prompt in other spheres. Most of our knowledge of these mines derives from the stamped metal ingots or pigs, weighing about 180 lb, which were made to facilitate transport. These show that the Mendip mines were in use in AD 49, only six years after the conquest, and that at first they were worked under a

Opposite, Roman London, *c.* AD 80: plan of the governor's palace or *praetorium*, complete with pools, fountains, and a prospect of the Thames.

London as it probably appeared in *c.* AD 100: a rapidly expanding port and trading centre, with a network of roads radiating across the new province.

military administration. One ingot was exported during Nero's reign to St Valéry-sur-Somme. In AD 60 an ingot found at Stockbridge, Hants, probably from the Mendips, records the existence of a civilian agent: NERONIS AUG. EX K. IAN. IIII COS. BRIT. EX ARGENT. C. NIPI ASCANI (The property of Nero Augustus, consul from 1st January for the fourth time. British lead from the silver workings of Gaius Nipius Ascanius). Ascanius later transferred his interests to Ciwyd (Flint), where

Mendip lead was being extracted within a decade of the Roman invasion, under imperial control. This ingot, found at Stockbridge, Hants, is slightly later, dating to AD 60.

his name occurs on an ingot which can hardly be earlier than the campaigns of Suetonius Paulinus; the earliest dated ingot from this field belongs to AD 74 and is inscribed DEGEANGLICIUM. There is also mention of an imperial freedman, Tiberius Claudius Triferna, who worked first in the Mendips in 69–79, but later appears at Lutudarum (Matlock?) in Derbyshire.

Tacitus' testimony to the spread of the more liberal arts, the speaking of Latin and the wearing of the toga (on official occasions of course, not every day by 'the man in the street') can be accepted as a fact, but cannot be illustrated in much chronological detail. We know, for instance, that one of the men employed by Agricola in his educational drive was probably a schoolmaster named Demetrius (see p. 147), but we cannot closely date the graffiti scrawled in Latin which help to show the spread of the language. It will, therefore, be better to consider cultural aspects later in their own contexts.

4

Defence: The second and third centuries

The continuing growth of town life, together with a generally more civilized quality, depended on adequate protection from the wilder tribes in the north. So although Agricola's conquests in northern Scotland were abandoned c. AD 87, a frontier was established along the Clyde–Forth line, and some forts south of this border were reconstructed in Lowland Scotland, as at Newstead on the Tweed. This position seems to have been maintained for more than a decade, but disturbances in Britain and pressures arising from his war against Dacia (Romania) induced the emperor Trajan to withdraw still further to a frontier along the Tyne–Solway line. Here he fortified the 'Stanegate' road with watch-towers and small forts, perhaps c. AD 105. He also strengthened the province itself, reconstructing in stone the three legionary fortresses at York, Chester and Caerleon, and building new forts in Wales and probably in London, namely the Cripplegate fort, northwest of the inhabited area. In addition, two new coloniae had already been established: at Lincoln, c. AD 90, and at Gloucester, 96–8.

Before very long, however, the tribes on both sides of Trajan's frontier line gave trouble – the Brigantes in the south and the Selgovae and Novantae in the north. These uprisings were suppressed by 118, but the new emperor Hadrian chose to apply the same defensive policy in Britain as in the rest of the empire, where he abandoned Trajan's conquests. In 122 he came to Britain himself, together with Platorius Nepos as governor, and a new legion, the VI Victrix, to replace IX Hispana. This latter legion mysteriously disappears from history. Once it was thought to have been wiped out in an insurrection in Britain, but it was more probably moved to the Continent and subsequently perished, perhaps in the Jewish war of 132. Hadrian then decided on the stupendous task of constructing a wall 80 miles long across Britain from the Tyne to the Solway; stupendous, since it involved quarrying and moving some 2,000,000 tons of rock and soil. Its purpose was to 'divide and rule', to split the Brigantes from the Selgovae by a permanent frontier line, as well as to protect the more civilized population further south.

As the building of the Wall proceeded, many changes of plan had to be made which the skilful detective work of modern archaeologists has brought to light, but which cannot be given in detail here. A large ditch, 27 feet wide and 10 feet deep, was dug in front (i.e. to the north) of the Wall, which was built by the legionaries themselves, with inscriptions recording the lengths put up by individual working parties. The whole length was a continuous stone structure, though at the beginning (perhaps until 158) the western part was constructed out of turf. It was never less than 8 feet thick and 15 feet high,

The emperor and his Wall: *above*, a realistic portrait head of Hadrian, found in the Thames at London. *Below*, Britannia guards the Wall on a Hadrianic *sestertius* of 134–8.

Opposite, Hadrian's Wall: the desolate landscape of the frontier at Walltown Crags, looking west.

Northern defences: *above*, a stretch of the Wall as it may have looked when newly completed. *Opposite below*, the fort at Housesteads, Northumberland, showing the line of the Wall running along the top, the military buildings inside the ramparts (which measure 610 × 367 feet), and traces of the civilian settlement at rear. *Opposite above*, Cawfields mile-castle, built by Legio II, shows Roman engineering skill in difficult terrain.

and at every mile there was a fortlet with gates to the front and rear providing ways through. Between each of these mile-castles were two watch-turrets some 20 feet square, while at regular intervals a series of 16 forts partly projected beyond the Wall. Behind this line a ditch (*vallum* or *fossatum*) was dug, 20 feet wide, 10 feet deep, and with a flat bottom of 8 feet. The upcast soil formed two mounds about 100 feet apart. Very recent discoveries have shown that defence works continued for many miles along the Cumbrian coast, at least as far as Ravenglass, consisting of mile-castles and watch-towers, but no walls. In order to man the Wall, the garrisons of some forts in Brigantian territory had to be reduced. In all, about 9,500 men were needed in the forts of the Wall, while the mile-castles were manned by three or four cohorts of auxiliaries in detachments (*vexillationes*) along its length.

The Wall may have had a parapet sentry walk, but this would not have been used as a fighting platform. Unlike a town wall, it had to provide a lookout in both directions, back as well as front, since its purpose was to split the enemy and to watch and control their movements. On occasion the Roman cavalry may perhaps have sallied forth from this strong base and rounded up parties of the enemy against the Wall itself, but such tactics are uncertain. The purpose of the *vallum* to the south is not clear, but it probably incorporated an earlier lateral trackway by which supplies could be distributed along the Wall. Its ditch, unlike the one in front of the Wall

itself, was not primarily built for military needs, but marked out the line of the military zone, and prevented unauthorized approach from the south.

Behind this northern shield the more civilized part of the province, it was hoped, could live in peace and increasing prosperity, but surprising variations of policy occurred under Hadrian's successors. Soon after his accession in 138, Antoninus Pius decided to move the frontier line back again up to the Forth–Clyde, and to modify the defensive nature of Hadrian's Wall by removing the gates from the mile-castles, and by building causeways across the *vallum*. This change of policy may have been caused by disturbances in south Scotland. At any rate, under the command of Lollius Urbicus men from the three legions built 37 miles of turf wall on a stone foundation from Forth to Clyde, with a *vallum* in front and a 'military way' (a road connecting the forts) behind. On it were some 19 forts spaced at two-mile intervals – closer together than the forts on Hadrian's Wall, and varying in size. Behind this wall lay a secure base at Newstead, and outlying forts (e.g. at Ardoch) covered it in the north. It was completed by or soon after AD 142, and its garrison, consisting mainly of cohorts of auxiliaries, was quartered in the forts. In proportion to the length of the two walls, the northern garrison was nearly twice as strong as that of Hadrian's Wall.

Uprisings followed in the 150s, but it is uncertain whether the Brigantes were involved or only tribes further north. One view is that, since the building of the Antonine Wall involved moving men from the forts in the Pennines, the Brigantes saw their chance to revolt but were crushed in the later 150s, when the governor Julius Verus opposed them with reinforcements which he had brought from Germany, and even with troops summoned from Scotland. Alternatively, the trouble may have been confined to the north and have been settled in the earlier 150s, before Verus' arrival. At all events, the Antonine Wall was apparently abandoned at about this time. Shortly afterwards, however, *c.* 158–63, it was once more occupied. Until recently this reoccupation was thought to have continued till 180, together with that of Hadrian's Wall, but this now seems less probable. Another possibility is that, since it failed to bring peace and further

The Antonine Wall: Britannia is again invoked on a *sestertius* of 143–4 celebrating the completion of the Wall. *Below*, a 'distance slab' from Bridgeness records a stretch of wall constructed by Legio II Augusta.

The Antonine Wall near the
Firth of Forth: *above*, a length
of Wall and Ditch near
Rough Castle (*below*), a tiny
post only one acre in extent
but fully equipped.

A cavalry parade helmet from Ribchester, Lancs, where a mounted force of Sarmatians (Slavs from the Danube area) was quartered towards the end of the second century.

disturbances occurred, in 162 the governor Calpurnius Agricola was sent out by Antoninus' successor, Marcus Aurelius, to crush the unrest and then to withdraw from Scotland, holding the line at Hadrian's Wall. So the Romans deliberately abandoned the Antonine Wall, burning its forts in order to deny them to the enemy, and Hadrian's Wall was once again put into full working order.

In 175 the garrison in Britain was strengthened by the arrival of over 5,000 Sarmatian cavalry, but in the first year of Commodus' reign (AD 180) disaster struck when, according to the historian Dio Cassius, the tribes of central Scotland overran 'the Wall'. On the assumption that the Antonine Wall had been abandoned some years earlier, this brief reference must be to Hadrian's Wall, where there is in fact evidence of some damage. The attack was crushed by Ulpius Marcellus, but Commodus showed no desire to return to a frontier line in Scotland. This decision left the tribes in the Lowlands greater freedom, and they united into a large confederacy of the Maeatae, while further north the Caledonians maintained their own confederacy.

But all was not well at the heart of the empire, where the central government was threatened by civil war between three contenders for supreme power: Decimus Clodius Albinus, governor of Britain, L. Septimius Severus in Pannonia (Hungary), and Pescennius Niger in Syria, each supported by his own army group. Septimius held Albinus at bay by granting him the title of Caesar and a free hand in Britain and the west, while he himself hastened to the east where he finally defeated Niger in 194. Meanwhile Albinus prepared for the inevitable war. Raised to the rank of Augustus by his troops, he led them across from Britain to France, where he was finally defeated by Septimius near Lyons and committed suicide in 197. Septimius remained undisputed master of the Roman world.

Rome's enemies in a Britain denuded of troops made the most of their chance. Caledonians and Maeatae broke through Hadrian's Wall and overran the north of England as far as York; disturbances erupted among the Brigantes and in Wales. Eventually the Brigantes were quelled and the northern invaders were bribed by the governor Virius Lupus (198–202) to withdraw to the north of the Wall, which had been so badly damaged that later generations thought Septimius responsible for its original building, when he had in fact only ordered its reconstruction, completed in 207 by L. Alfenus Senecio. The long delay may have been due to continued disturbances in the Pennines, or even (according to a recent theory) to the possibility that Lupus was ordered to punish the Maeatae by renewed annexation. But if this was so, the attempt was soon abandoned, and by 205 Senecio was reconstructing Hadrian's frontier.

Septimius, however, was not content with a defensive policy in Britain. In 208 he arrived in Britain in person, although 63 years old, with the empress Julia Domna and his two sons Caracalla and Geta, to launch an offensive in the north. Supported by his fleet, he advanced north to Aberdeen and the Moray Firth (a line of his marching camps survives) in an attempt to crush the Caledonians, while in the next year he campaigned against the Maeatae (his camps in 209 were larger than those of 208). But neither Septimius nor Caracalla could force the natives to meet them in a pitched battle, and so when Septimius died at York in February 211 his sons gave up any thought of re-establishing the line of the Antonine Wall, and evacuated Scotland. Hadrian's Wall remained the frontier of the province (or rather provinces, since in 197 Britain had been divided into Britannia Superior and Britannia Inferior). The *vallum* however was not restored, and the gateways of the mile-castles were narrowed. Outpost forts, on the other hand, were brought back into repair, as at Risingham (Habitancum) and High Rochester (Bremenium). Their garrisons included detachments of scouts (*numeri speculatorum*) and more cavalry, so that a general supervision could be exercised over the Scottish Lowlands. In Wales, too, where there are traces of destruction at the end of the second century (e.g. at Brecon and Caerhun), reconstruction followed.

Septimius' campaigns can be regarded as failures if his objective was the permanent conquest of Scotland (as hostile sources represented), but if his aim was limited to a massive punitive expedition and the restoration of the *status quo*, then they were far from unsuccessful: the northern frontier enjoyed peace for much of the rest of the century, while civilian life within the protected province took a fresh turn when Caracalla granted Roman citizenship to all free inhabitants of the Roman empire, including Britain.

During the mid-third century, however, the empire was heading for collapse until Diocletian finally restored order in 284. The central authority was undermined as various armies put forward a whole series of claimants to the throne, many of whom were quickly murdered; rampant inflation caused the economic structure to crack and nearly to crumble; the northern and eastern frontiers were overrun by barbarians and Persians. Marcus Postumus, a commander on the Rhine who beat back some Franks and Alamanni, managed in 259 to create an independent empire based on Gaul, which was joined by Spain and Britain and lasted until it was finally overthrown by Aurelian (in 273) who justly gained the title of *restitutor orbis* (Restorer of the World) by his victories in both west and east.

Britain was protected from the worst of the troubles that struck the Roman empire, thanks to her remote position beyond the Channel. Yet she did have to face one increasing danger, that of Saxon pirates and raiders. Until the third century the seas had been adequately patrolled by a fleet, the *classis Britannica*. This had at first been based at Boulogne, with its main British port probably at Richborough, but in the 80s Dover became more important. Besides providing the army in Britain with transport and supplies, the fleet patrolled the seas on both sides of the Channel.

Richborough (Rutupiae), Kent, beach-head of the original Roman invasion of AD 43, and subsequently a fort of the Saxon Shore. The cross shape inside the walls marks the base of a vast triumphal arch erected in the first century.

Camouflage was used to enable it to pounce on marauders, according to Vegetius, a late military writer, who reports that scouting vessels had blue sails and the sailors wore blue uniforms.

However, the need for more land-based protection was gradually felt, and so before (perhaps well before) the middle of the third century forts had been established at Reculver in Kent to protect the Thames estuary, and at Brancaster in East Anglia to cover the Wash. Then followed a series of some twelve forts, the so-called forts of the Saxon Shore, which ultimately spread a protective shield from Brancaster to Portchester near Portsmouth. Until quite recently it was believed that they were all built as a unitary defence system devised by the usurper Carausius (AD 286–93), but it is now thought that they came into being as need compelled. Burgh, Bradwell, Richborough, Dover, and Lympne appear to date from around the 270s, and perhaps the emperor Probus (276–82) should be given credit for them. Carausius, however, may have been responsible for Portchester, which seems slightly later, while Pevensey arose in response to much later raids, perhaps in the 340s. One of the main purposes of these forts was to bar the Straits of Dover to Saxon and other raiders, and so block access to the richer parts of southern England. In consequence, both sides of the Channel were still guarded, with forts on the continental shore at Boulogne and at Oudenberg in Belgium. From about the middle of the third century the *classis Britannica* is no longer recorded as a unit, while its base at Dover had been abandoned about 200: its place was taken in the second half of the third century by a fort

Portchester, near Portsmouth: a very well-preserved fort of the Saxon Shore with massive walls and hollow bastions which once contained heavy artillery.

Marcus Aurelius Carausius, appointed naval commander in the Channel, seized power in Britain, 286–93.

of the Saxon Shore. Nearly all these Shore forts have massive stone walls, about 30 feet high, defended by projecting bastions; they are rectangular and enclose some six to ten acres. The remains of those at Richborough and Portchester are among the most impressive buildings in Roman Britain.

To meet the Saxon challenge the emperor Maximian entrusted the Channel naval command to M. Aurelius Mausaeus Carausius, but later ordered his death when he found that Carausius was lining his own pockets with the booty he recovered from the raiders. Carausius promptly sought refuge in Britain (286–7), where he gained the support of the troops, doubtless by generous use of his spoils from the Saxons, and established an independent kingdom which included part of northern Gaul. This he continued to hold for some years, since Maximian and Diocletian were busy reshaping the Roman empire and establishing the new system of the tetrarchy, under which the government was shared by two Augusti and two junior Caesars. This meant that when Carausius in 290 claimed to be a colleague of the other two emperors, he was seeking recognition as a Roman emperor rather than merely asserting himself as ruler of an independent Britain. But he ruled well, controlling the army effectively, helping the economy with his extensive coinage, and continuing the strategy of the Saxon Shore forts.

In 293, however, after losing Boulogne to the Caesar Constantius, Carausius was assassinated and supplanted by his own finance minister Allectus, against whom Constantius mounted an invasion in 296. While Constantius himself created a diversion in the Channel, his praetorian prefect Asclepiodotus eluded the enemy fleet in a fog, landed near

Southampton Water, and defeated Allectus near Silchester. Constantius' forces sailed up the Thames and saved London from some of Allectus' defeated troops who were about to attack the city. The triumphal arrival of Constantius, styled *redditor lucis aeternae* (Restorer of Eternal Light) and the personified figure of Londinium (perhaps now given the title Caesarea) are depicted on the famous gold medallion found near Arras (see p. 141). Thus Britain was reunited within the Roman empire.

Reconstruction followed. The two provinces of Britannia were divided, perhaps into three and then (before 312–14) certainly into four provinces. After a long period of peace the north again received attention. Constantius may have taken the field against the Picts (Caledonians) in 296, as he certainly did when he returned to Britain in 306 and reached the far north of Scotland. This may have been a pre-emptive strike, but more probably was a punitive measure in response to an attack on the Wall: it may well be that the northerners had seized their opportunity when Allectus withdrew some troops from the north in order to face Constantius. At all events the Wall with its mile-castles and turrets was repaired, together with the outlying northern forts, and renovation of the defences of some southerly settlements (including probably York and Chester), which had suffered from neglect rather than destruction by the enemy, proceeded more gradually. Constantius, who had been brilliantly successful in his northern campaign, returned to York where he died. It was here that the army proclaimed his son Constantine as Augustus in his place. Constantine soon had to leave Britain to fight for his title, which he finally vindicated at the battle of the Mulvian Bridge in Rome in 312, but before he left he repaired many roads (six milestones belong to these months), thus following up his father's policy of consolidation and giving Britain a further period of great peace and prosperity.

5

Military and civil administration

THE ARMY

The pacification and defence of Britain required a permanent presence of some 55,000 Roman troops, but these men also profoundly affected the development of social and economic life, stimulating economic needs and introducing new cultural and religious ideas. Today we are still reminded of their activities in the striking remains of their camps and fortifications, while a very considerable proportion of inscriptions found in Roman Britain record their careers and service. They, therefore, deserve closer inspection, the more so since they were not a monolithic block but individuals of very varied races and creeds. They were far from being pure 'Romans' in the sense of deriving from Rome, or even Italy, but belonged to many nationalities and came from many parts of the Roman empire. Indeed during the first two centuries AD about half of them were not even Roman citizens.

The army comprised two separate groups: the legionaries and the auxiliaries (*auxilia*). The legions consisted of Roman citizens, drawn from Italy and the more civilized provinces such as Gaul or Spain, and serving for 20 years. Each legion was made up of about 5,500 men, including 120 horsemen, and bore a number and a title, e.g. Legio VI Victrix. It was divided into 10 cohorts, each subdivided into 6 units called centuries. The legion was commanded by a *legatus legionis*, a Roman senator who had reached the rank of praetor. His staff consisted of 6 military tribunes, whose military service formed an early stage in a political career. In battle the effective leadership was given by the 59 centurions, tough professional soldiers who had generally risen from the ranks. They, like their cohorts, were graded according to seniority. The chief centurion (*primus pilus*) had great authority and served on the staff of the legate, while the second centurion (*princeps*) controlled the administrative staff.

The auxiliary forces were recruited from the wilder frontier provinces and were not usually Roman citizens, though they were given this status after 25 years' service. On discharge their citizenship was recorded on bronze diplomas (see p. 76). Their units were smaller than those of the legions, and consisted of infantry cohorts or cavalry *alae*, both of which were theoretically grouped in units of 500 (*quingenariae*) or less usually 1,000 men (*milliariae*). The cohorts, each commanded by a Roman prefect (*praefectus cohortis*), were either entirely infantrymen (*peditatae*) or else included a mounted contingent of 120 (*equitatae*), and like the legions were divided into centuries commanded by centurions. The cavalry *ala* was commanded by a prefect and divided into squadrons (*turmae*) of 16 or 24 men, each commanded by a *decurio*.

Opposite, Roman legionaries at work in a tableau from Trajan's Column, Rome. Wall-building was an important part of the soldiers' duties, and one which has had far-reaching effects on the British landscape.

The auxiliary troops were brigaded with the legions, but were kept distinct from them. They were armed more lightly and were employed partly as skirmishers and specialist troops, such as cavalry, archers and slingers. After the mid-first century AD they seldom served in the country where they were raised, but were posted to other provinces. Their origin was often commemorated in their titles (e.g. Cohors I Hispanorum from Spain, II Pannoniorum from Hungary), though occasionally they retained the name of the man who had raised them, as in the case of Ala Siliana, raised by C. Silius. Thus at first we find men from many nations serving in Roman Britain, but in the course of time the ethnic character was weakened through the necessity of local recruiting – it was not always possible to summon replacements from a distant country of origin. Drafts from home seem to have kept up the numbers of the Oriental cohorts of archers, but some local recruitment in Britain may have started as early as the 80s for the *auxilia*, and in the mid-second century for legionaries.

When Caracalla granted Roman citizenship to the whole empire in 211, one main distinction between legionaries and auxiliaries disappeared and the latter declined. Gradually, and more particularly in the third century, a new type of national levy was developed, units called *numeri* which had to serve in frontier areas far distant from their homelands. Thus we find Mesopotamians, Moors and Sarmatians serving in Britain, and British *numeri* (raised in southern Scotland) on the German frontier. These *numeri* seem to have retained their national identities to a greater extent than the auxiliaries. But by this time the nature of the whole Roman army was changing, as we shall see later (p. 171).

Besides the legions and *auxilia* there were the crack troops of the Praetorian Guard, essentially a corps attached to the emperor. This was stationed in Rome and Italy, but detachments could accompany an emperor abroad; Claudius, for instance, brought some to Britain when he crossed the Channel in AD 43.

Numerous inscriptions illustrated the careers of soldiers. One of the best pieces of sculpture in Roman Britain is the tombstone of M. Favonius, who died at Colchester before AD 60. He is shown standing, bareheaded, with corslet and kilt, armed with sword and dagger, and carrying the vine staff which was the centurion's symbol of power to flog. The inscription simply records: 'Marcus Favonius Facilis, son of Marcus, of the tribe of Pollia [all Roman citizens were registered in one of 35 groups called tribes], centurion of Legio XX. Verecundus and Narcissus his freedmen set up this. Here he lies.'

More spectacular was the career of M. Vettius Valens, who served twice in Britain. An honorary dedication made to him at Ariminum (Rimini) in Italy in AD 66 proclaims that he had been a soldier in Cohors VIII of the Praetorian Guard, attached to the staff of the prefect of the Guard, and had received military decorations (neck-chains, medals and armlets) in the British war (*bello Britannico*). After 16 years' service (the normal length for a Guardsman) Valens had enlisted again as a veteran (*evocatus Augusti*) and had a distinguished career, including service in Rome as centurion of Cohors VI of the Vigiles and of Cohors XVI of the Urban Cohorts. He next became second senior centurion (*princeps praetorii*) of Legio XIII Gemina in

Opposite, Marcus Favonius Facilis, centurion of Legio XX at Colchester in the earliest days of the conquest. His tombstone, found there and dated to before AD 60, emphasizes his rank.

A Roman military diploma from Dacia, showing British units.

Pannonia (Hungary), then probably chief centurion (*primus pilus*) in Legio VI Victrix in York. After receiving further decorations for campaigns against the Asturians in northwest Spain, he reached the rank of tribune, a very rare achievement for an ex-private. Having held the post of tribune in the Vigiles, Urban Cohorts and Praetorian Guard, he returned to Britain as tribune of Legio XIV Gemina Martia Victrix. Finally he served in Lusitania (Portugal) as imperial procurator (financial officer), responsible to the emperor Nero, and then in his fifties he retired, having become a Roman knight (*eques*) and 'patron' of the colony at Ariminum. His descendants there later became Roman senators, while one, perhaps a grandson, even became 'patron of the province of Britain'.

Tiberius Flavius Virilis, a third-century soldier, not only served as a centurion in Britain but was probably British himself. He was centurion successively in the legions stationed at Caerleon, Chester and York, and then once again at Chester. Afterwards he was posted to the legion at Lambaesis in North Africa, where he later died aged 70, after 45 years of somewhat undistinguished service. His funeral monument was erected by his wife Lollia Bodicca and his two sons. Her names are interesting, since Lollia was a Latin family name and may suggest that her family had received Roman citizenship from Lollius Urbicus, the governor of Britain 141–3, while her other name is a version of Boudicca, the earlier queen of the Iceni.

Auxiliary soldiers' names are recorded on tombstones and diplomas. Of the former a simple example comes from Gloucester: 'Rufus Sita, trooper of the Sixth Thracian Cohort, aged 40 with 22 years' service. His heirs set this up, according to his will. Here he lies.' When auxiliary regiments were discharged, the relevant imperial edict was set up in bronze in Rome, while

Opposite, the Cirencester tombstone of a Thracian trooper, Valerius Genialis, who served there, and was a Frisian by birth.

75

Dover lighthouse (*pharos*), which probably dates from the second century, was octagonal in plan, and originally stood about 80 feet high.

individual soldiers could have copies made to keep as certificates of their newly granted citizenship. These diplomas consisted of two bronze plaques, folded together, tied and sealed, which quoted the edict in full but gave only the name of the individual soldier. They provide invaluable evidence for the distribution of the auxiliary units throughout the empire. Part of one, found at Malpas near Chester and bearing a date equivalent to 19 January 103, may be quoted:

The emperor Trajan . . . to the cavalry and infantry serving in the four *alae* and eleven cohorts [the units are then named] who are now serving in Britain under Lucius Neratius Marcellus, and have served not less than 25 years, and whose names appear below, has granted citizenship for themselves, their children and their posterity, and rights of marriage with the wives whom they had when citizenship was granted to them, or in the case of unmarried men with those whom they may thereafter have married; but not more than one wife to one man. This copy belongs to Reburrus, son of Severus, the Spaniard, *decurio* in Tampius' First Pannonian *ala*, commanded by C. Valerius Celsus.

The units named had originally been raised in a variety of countries – Gaul, Spain, the Rhineland, Belgium and Dalmatia – but the extent to which they had been diluted at this time by local recruiting remains uncertain: Reburrus, a Spaniard, was serving in a unit originally consisting of Pannonians from Hungary!

Nor should we forget the navy, the *classis Britannica* which, especially before the Saxon menace demanded more frequent patrolling of the coasts, provided a valuable back-up service for the army, and even seems to have helped with the iron industry in the Weald of Kent and Sussex. It cooperated in some campaigns, especially those of Agricola and Septimius Severus, and secured transport and supplies. An inscription from Benwell on the Tyne records that the navy supplied a landing party (*vexillatio*) to help in connection with the building of Hadrian's Wall: 'To the emperor Caesar Traianus Hadrianus Augustus, a detachment of the British fleet [built this] under Aulus Platorius Nepos, governor.' Another Hadrianic inscription from Lympne (Portus Lemanis) records, 'Lucius Aufidius Pantera, commander [*praefectus*] of the British fleet [dedicated] this altar to Neptune.' M. Maenius Agrippa, perhaps a successor to Aufidius as naval commander, came from a small Italian village and enjoyed a very successful career, recorded with gratitude and pride in a memorial put up by the villagers. He had served in Britain or commanded British troops no less than four times: 'Commander of Vespasian's Own Second part-cavalry Cohort, chosen by the emperor Hadrian and sent on the British expedition, tribune commanding Cohors I Equitata of Spaniards [this was stationed in Britain, and while in command of it Maenius dedicated no less than four altars to Jupiter at Alauna, near Maryport in Cumberland], commander of the British fleet, and procurator of the province of Britain.' The inscription also records that Maenius was father of a senator and himself a knight (*equo publico*) – a good illustration of the degree of social mobility in the Roman empire.

In the second century, as recent excavations in the 1970s have shown, the headquarters of the fleet was probably at Dover where its fort has been found,

together with some 800 tiles stamped CL(ASSIS) BR(ITANNICA). The fort was over two acres in area and enclosed barracks and granaries; some of its walls survive to the height of three metres. The buildings of an extramural civilian settlement include the now famous 'Painted House', with much of its brightly decorated plaster still *in situ*. In the third century this fort was replaced by a Saxon Shore fort, which was built slightly overlapping the older site. This, too, is a recent discovery, and is still (1978) being investigated. Dover also possesses a unique monument in the Roman lighthouse (*pharos*) which still stands about 43 feet high, with another 20 feet of medieval rebuilding on top; it originally rose to some 80 feet, and guided all shipping in the Channel with smoke by day and fire by night. It was matched by a second, later lighthouse, of which only the stub remains, on the Western Heights.

The prime purpose of the Roman army was, of course, to fight when needed, and this it did supremely well. British tribesmen, however courageous, had little chance of success against it in a pitched battle. As regards equipment, the men wore metal helmets, and their bodies were protected with articulated plate armour. Two sets of this, found in 1964 at Corbridge on Hadrian's Wall, have resolved the old problem of how this

A Roman galley. To counter the Saxon threat, the Romans maintained a substantial naval presence in the Channel.

Models of a legionary (*left*) and a praetorian in full military regalia.

armour was constructed. The shield was rectangular and made of layers of wood and leather, with a metal boss in the centre. One such boss, belonging to Junius Dubitatus, who served in Britain with a detachment of Legio VIII Augusta in the second century, has been rescued from the river Tyne. The leather apron had metal discs, and the leather sandals had iron-studded soles. From the belt hung the short, double-bladed, pointed sword and dagger. The legionary also carried two javelins (*pila*). These he hurled at the enemy and then rushed in to hand-to-hand fighting with the sword, at which he was highly expert. His training also included a 19-mile route march nearly every week, drill once or twice a day, which was directed by a drill instructor (*armatura*: one such made a dedication found at Lydney, Glos.), and instruction in swimming and stone-slinging. He had to be able to vault on to a horse (stirrups had not been invented), and to mount and dismount fully armed with shield and equipment. He was also required to dig, and to build a camp, and in fact he developed great technical skill in handling and moving earth, turf, timber and stone.

In the early days of conquest, the more lightly armed auxiliaries were chiefly required to back up the legions, on whom the brunt of the fighting

Opposite, bronze centreplate of a legionary's shield, found in the river Tyne.

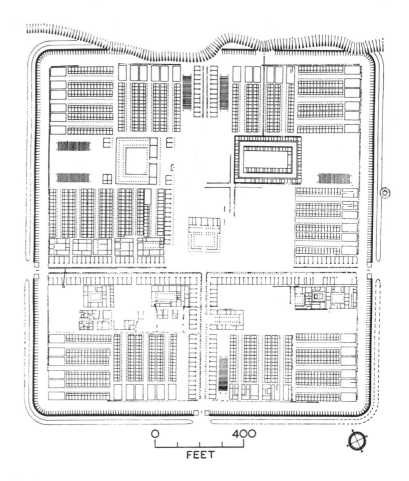

The unfinished legionary fortress at Inchtuthil, Perthshire (AD 83–6) comprised 53 acres and included headquarters, barracks, stores, granaries, parade ground and a military hospital.

O   400

FEET

fell, but at the battle of Mons Graupius Agricola used them as front-line troops, keeping his legions back as a reserve. Thereafter the Walls were manned primarily by the *auxilia*, while the legions were kept back in the three great fortresses at York, Chester and Caerleon, from where they could advance or send out detachments to any danger points.

Construction of the great fortresses, smaller forts, and temporary marching camps was a major task for the troops. The requisite skills had to be gained by practice, and many earthworks still survive which were clearly built for this purpose alone, both smaller works erected by auxiliaries in Wales, especially on Llandrindrod Common, and larger efforts built by legionaries, for instance in Yorkshire.

The standard plan of the headquarters fortresses is best shown at Inchtuthil and Caerleon. The camp covered 50 acres or more, and housed some 6,000 men. The layout and complex buildings can be seen in the illustrations. Within the enclosing ditches and rampart, the area was laid out with the general's quarters (*praetorium*) and HQ buildings (*principia*) as the pivot. It was crossed by a main roadway (*via principalis*) and flanked by the tribunes' quarters. Another street, the *via praetoria*, formed a T-junction with the *via principalis*.

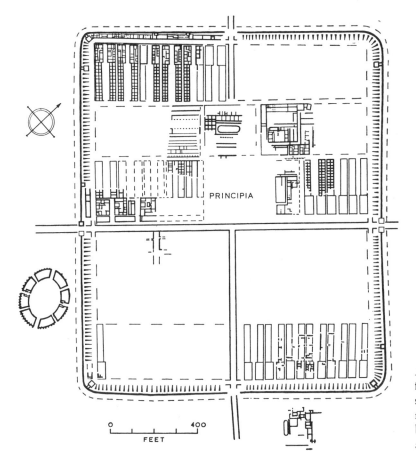

PRINCIPIA

FEET
0   400

A plan of the legionary
fortress at Caerleon, Gwent,
shows the HQ (*principia*) and a
number of excavated barrack
buildings inside the 50-acre
area of the ramparts.

The troops were quartered in barrack blocks along streets at right angles to
the *via principalis*. Hospitals, granaries, bath-houses and workshops were
provided. Outside were amphitheatres (at Chester and Caerleon) for
training and entertainment, and parade grounds. Traders tended to
congregate near the camp; shops, inns, temples and private houses sprang up,
and civil towns gradually developed. Here the families of the garrison might
live, children be born, and veterans settle. These *vici* or *canabae* provided a
source from which, in the second century, many legionaries were recruited.

Smaller forts were required for the smaller units, especially the auxiliaries
stationed throughout the defensive zones of the country. They were sited at
strategic positions, often on a small plateau at a river junction, and varied in
size according to need. The average fort for a quingenary cohort was about
three and a half acres, while the milliary cohort occupied five. Under Trajan
and Hadrian, stone was increasingly used to replace earlier turf walls and
timber buildings. These earlier forts were designed to garrison troops whose
function was to fight in the open: hence their wide gateways and a rampart
walk for observation. Later the gates were made higher and narrower, with
bastions to enfilade attackers, and artillery platforms (*ballistaria*), and the
rampart walk developed into a defensible fighting platform. As R.G.

Roman roads were often constructed by the legionaries themselves. A detail from Trajan's Column.

Collingwood pointed out, the 'little camp' (*castellum*) was moving towards its medieval meaning of 'castle'.

Numerous Roman forts survive, from the Claudian period – e.g. at Margidunum near Nottingham – down to the large defensive forts of the Saxon Shore. There are also a number of examples in Wales, where the Flavian earthworks are shown to have been replaced by second-century stonework, as at Brecon Gaer in the south, Castell Collen in Powys, Tomen-y-Mur high in the wild mountains of Gwynedd, Caerhun (Canovium) in the quieter Conway valley, and Caernarvon (Segontium) facing Anglesey.

Whenever a Roman army was on the march, especially in enemy territory, it always built an entrenched camp for the night, where the men slept in leather tents within the safety of the earthworks and palisades. Since the camp layout was standardized, each man knew exactly where his quarters lay and the camp could be set up in quick time and in good order. Many of these marching-camps are known, a considerable number having been revealed by air photography. They survive in southern England, through Wales and in the north, with a string up the east side of Scotland (these last being Agricolan or Severan).

Beside the normal duties and fatigues of camp life, the soldier had not only to build his camp but also to undertake the backbreaking work of road-building, quarrying and canal-digging, tasks which fell, unexpectedly, to the legionaries rather than to the auxiliaries. Thus it was the legions, not auxiliaries or native levies, who built Hadrian's Wall, as numerous 'centurial' stones attest. These reveal details of construction as each unit finished its task: for example, 'The century of Claudius built 30½ feet', or 'The century of Primus built 112 feet of rampart under the command of Flavius Secundus, the prefect.' The legionaries also made their own tiles (stamped with the legionary title) and much of their pottery. At Holt, 12 miles south of Chester, the tile and pottery factory of Legio XX covered some 20 acres. Similar works, on a smaller scale, are found in many auxiliary forts. Outside the fort at Catterick a tannery was worked from c. AD 80–120: the armies needed great quantities of leather for uniforms, boots and tents. Timber, another requirement, was probably prepared at the camp. It is estimated that 7 miles of timber walls were needed for the framework of the barracks at Inchtuthil, where no less than 11 tons of unused iron nails were found, while we know that metalworking was carried out at Corbridge. Whether the legionaries themselves did all the hard work in these industrial activities, or in part only supervised them, we cannot say. Additional supplies, of course, would be produced in the civil settlements outside the camp, perhaps sometimes under contract. This reminds us that the presence of so many troops in Britain created and stimulated fresh economic needs.

One of the army's main concerns was its food supply, much of which came from civilian sources, either by purchase at a fixed price or by requisitioning under the tax system. In addition to the basic rations, which were supplied officially against stoppages of pay, an individual soldier could buy extras from civilian producers or traders in the neighbouring *vicus*. The army in Britain, according to recent calculations, needed annually some 530,000 bushels of corn, the produce of 306,000 acres. An analysis of animal bones found in Roman forts in Britain and Germany shows that, contrary to the conventional view, the army ate considerable quantities of meat – ox, sheep, pork and goats – as well as cereals, cheese, and vegetables, especially beans and lentils; poultry, fish and shellfish where available, and fruits and nuts. A poor quality sour wine (*acetum*), often mixed with water, was drunk, but vintage wine (*vinum*) was also imported, as shown by names written in ink on the necks of amphorae: one of these in the wine cellars of the military stores depot at Richborough mentions a wine from Mount Vesuvius. Caerleon received a high quality Aminean wine, and a vessel at Mumrills contained 'sweet wine' (so labelled in Greek); Celtic beer was also popular.

Interesting light has recently been thrown on this military diet by some documents, found in the pre-Hadrianic fort at Vindolanda, written with a reed pen on slivers of thin wood which have been preserved, thanks to an unusual chemical condition of the soil and bracken where they were found. Some contain records of the issues of food over a period of several days in June

Two leaves of a writing-tablet, part of a letter of recommendation found at Vindolanda, Northumberland, and dated earlier than AD 105.

around the year AD 100, listing barley (which was generally fed to animals), Celtic beer, vintage wine and *acetum*, a fish sauce (*muria*), and pork fat (*axungia*). There is also a reference to some religious matter (*ad sacrum*), which may mean special food supplies for a festival. Another fragment refers to spice, goat's meat, salt, young pig, ham, corn and a 'white corn' (*bracis*).

We know from papyri letters in Egypt that Roman soldiers often wrote home to their relatives asking for extra food. No doubt they did so in Britain also, and Vindolanda has yielded fragments of a private letter covering the sending of additional clothing: 'I have sent you [?] pairs of socks and for Sattia [?], two pairs of sandals; and two pairs of underpants [*subligariorum*], two pairs of sandals . . . greet my friend [?], Elpis, Tetricus and all your messmates; I pray that you and they may enjoy long life and the best of fortune.' It is noteworthy that several well-preserved sandals have actually been found at Vindolanda. Also no fewer than 14 *styli* (pens) were discovered in one room, which suggests that it may have been a record office.

The Roman soldier was engaged in many other activities besides fighting, which generally filled only a small part of his career on the island. These activities varied in effort according to his rank: a man with sufficient ability and education might seek a post giving him exemption from fatigues (*immunitas*), such as attachment to the commander's staff as a clerk (*librarius*), or on general duties (*beneficarius*). Alternatively, he might become a hospital orderly (*medicus*), a trumpeter or a bugler. Officers naturally fared better, and a legionary commander had almost palatial quarters in his *praetorium*. A wealthy Roman senator, he would be likely to take with him to the province as much as he could of his family, servants and household goods – Julius Caesar himself kept in his tent in Gaul a mosaic pavement transported from

Opposite, a Roman *medicus* (hospital orderly) attends a wounded soldier. Detail from Trajan's Column.

A gaming-board, counters, die and dicebox from Vindolanda. The die was discovered to be in perfect condition but loaded.

the homeland. The legionary commander's house was arranged round a central court, with a dining-room (*triclinium*) at the back, a bathroom, one wing for the family, and the other for the servants and the kitchen. At the rear there was a garden. Similar quarters on a smaller scale are found in the lesser forts, a good example being Fendoch in Scotland.

Officers could indulge in the comfort of a hot bath in almost 'Mediterranean' housing conditions, but a Syrian auxiliary, far from his Oriental homeland, must have regarded service in Britain in a somewhat different light, especially when, after a night's sentry duty, he gazed out from the Wall at dawn over the wild windswept desolation stretching away ever northwards into hostile territory. But life was not all bad: he could crowd into the centrally heated bath-house, just outside the fort, where men found warmth and relaxation. Dedications to the goddess Luck (Fortuna) are often found in or near bath-houses, and it is probable that the buildings were used as gambling clubs. Bone gaming counters may have been used – 12 were found in 1971 at Bermondsey in London. At Great Chesters (Aesica) on Hadrian's Wall an inscription on an altar records: 'To the goddess Fortuna, the detachment of Raetian Spearmen, under the command of Tabellius Victor, centurion, set this up.'

Country sports, especially hunting, were also popular when the season permitted, and sportsmen organized themselves into clubs (*collegia*). Thus the *Venatores Bannienses*, the Huntsmen of Banna (probably Bewcastle near the Wall), made a dedication to the country god Silvanus, and there is a well-known inscription recording a certain Veturius' pig-sticking triumph: 'To the unconquerable Silvanus: Gaius Tetius Veturius Micianus, prefect of the Sebosian Cavalry Regiment, on the fulfilment of his vow gladly set up this for the capture of a magnificent wild boar which many of his predecessors had failed to catch.'

THE GOVERNOR AND HIS STAFF

As an imperial province, Britain was governed by a representative of the emperor, to whom he was directly responsible. Entitled *legatus Augusti pro praetore* (legate of the emperor with propraetorian status), he was an ex-consul and a man of very considerable experience and distinction. The governors, who generally held office for three to five years, were carefully chosen by the emperors from among the most successful legionary commanders, men who had been trained in warfare (often on the Rhine–Danube frontier). In addition to the unofficial help of a group of friends (*cohors amicorum*), the governor had an administrative staff, which was commanded by a centurion (*princeps praetorii*) and included various grades of personnel, together with a clerical staff of slaves or freedmen. In his legal and financial administration he was aided by a *iuridicus* and a procurator, whose functions are discussed below, while in the exercise of his military duties he was, of course, the superior officer of the three legionary commanders. His administrative headquarters were probably moved to London before AD 60, as we have seen, and can be identified, as can the treasury offices of the procurator, while later his guard was probably stationed in the Cripplegate fort.

The official procuratorial stamp on a London writing-tablet makes clear that the city was the financial capital of the province.

The governor had exacting legal duties, but these were mainly in the criminal field since only the very important civil cases would come before him. But his was the final court in all cases involving non-citizens, and as the number of Roman citizens in the province increased, his judicial work swelled. In criminal cases citizens could appeal direct to Caesar from his judgment, and in the second century most capital cases, after a preliminary sifting by the governor, would normally be referred to Rome for the emperor's decision. The position was complicated by the fact that only Roman citizens were bound by Roman law, while the natives still lived under their Celtic codes. The gradual expansion of the province and occupation of new areas would inevitably involve legal questions, not least in the sphere of taxation. So, probably under Vespasian, the governor was provided with a subordinate legal officer, the *iuridicus*, who was also responsible to the emperor. We know the names of five such *iuridici* in Britain, two at least of whom were very distinguished lawyers. One, L. Iavolenus Priscus, served in Britain before his consulship of 86, probably under Agricola. An inscription from Dalmatia records that before he became *iuridicus provinciae Britanniae* Iavolenus had held two legionary commands, and later he governed Upper Germany, Syria and Africa, thus reaching the highest rung in a senatorial career.

The governor's authority, as we have seen, was not left unchecked: financial matters were entrusted to a procurator who would normally cooperate with him but was legally independent, and responsible direct to the emperor alone. Provincial governors must not be allowed unlimited power lest they become a threat to the central authority at Rome. Relations between the two men might vary. Tacitus praises Agricola for avoiding quarrelling with the procurators, but Julius Classicianus, who objected to Suetonius' ruthless punitive measures after the suppression of Boudicca's revolt, reported to the emperor adversely about the governor and so secured his recall.

The procurator was a member of the equestrian, not the senatorial, order at Rome. Augustus had made a sharp distinction between these two social orders, providing both with the opportunity for a progressive career in public service within the framework of an ordered pattern of promotion. The senatorial order filled military posts, while the equestrians were mainly civil servants (although at an early stage they had to hold three army postings). The *procurator Britanniae* was responsible for finance and taxation. He issued the army pay, received the taxes, and looked after any imperial property in the province, such as mines or estates. The revenue comprised two main taxes, one based on land (*tributum soli*), and the other a poll tax (*tributum capitis*), together with levies in kind, the *annona*, paid in grain for the upkeep of the army, and indirect taxes as harbour dues (*portoria*). The land tax required a census which would include details of production and ownership, whether of private, communal or state property. Hence periodic censuses were taken. These were the responsibility of the procurator and his HQ staff based in London, where a wooden writing-tablet has been found with the words 'issued by the imperial procurators of the province of Britain' (*procc. Aug. Brit. Prov. dederunt*). The staff needed supplementing at times, and we know of the appointment of special officials. T. Statius, for instance, was *procurator Augusti ad census Britanniae*, and had held a similar office in Gaul. A special *censitor*, Cn. Munatius Aurelius Bassus, was appointed to deal with the Roman citizens at Colchester, and he may have been especially seconded for this purpose since he also commanded Cohors II Asturum on Hadrian's Wall. Thirdly, we have T. Haterius Nepos, who was *censitor Brittonum Anavionensium*, probably in northern Britain. He later rose to the great dignity of becoming prefect of Egypt in AD 119–24. Tacitus records that the Britons paid their taxes promptly, provided abuses were absent. Unfortunately abuses were often only too prevalent, though good governors like Agricola did their best to stamp out the graft and corruption of minor officials.

The well-being of the province obviously depended on the efficiency and benevolence of the administrators. The rapacity of one procurator, Catus Decianus, had helped to precipitate the uprising of Boudicca; the moderation of another, Julius Classicianus, had helped to soften Roman retribution. Above all, the whole apparatus of government must have taken its tone from the character of the governors, which naturally varied considerably: Suetonius Paulinus had proved an efficient but ruthless soldier;

his successor Petronius Turpilianus acted with restraint. Trebellius Maximus who followed him was slacker, lacked military experience, and kept control of the province by a 'certain courtesy' (*comitate quadam*), as Tacitus reports, although his lack of discipline led to a mutiny in the army at a time when Rome itself was distracted by civil war. After the governorship of two highly competent soldiers came Agricola, the ideal governor, at least according to his biographer.

LOCAL GOVERNMENT: ROMAN AND NATIVE TOWNS

The Romans, as we have seen (pp. 47 ff.), tried to solve the problem of local government through a policy of urbanization. A few *coloniae* were founded for veteran legionaries and their families, and these of course enjoyed the full rights of Roman citizenship: Colchester first, and then, in the two decades before AD 100, Lincoln and Gloucester. Considerably later the settlement which had grown up outside the legionary fortress at York also received the honorary title of *colonia*. In addition, a very few towns were raised to the status of *municipia*, which entailed partial citizens' rights. These included St Albans and probably London, and just possibly, by the third century, even some tribal capitals such as Canterbury, Cirencester, Dorchester, Leicester and Wroxeter. But *coloniae* and *municipia* could not be created in large numbers, so the widespread basis of provincial administration was provided by establishing an increasing number of native *civitates* out of the existing village and tribal system. These were the channels through which the governors and procurators worked, and in consequence they were allowed to retain the right of local self-government, undertaking census surveys, collecting taxes and similar tasks.

The constitutions of the *coloniae* and *municipia*, which controlled a fairly wide area (*territorium*) around the town itself, were established by a foundation charter (*lex coloniae*) and were modelled on Rome.

They had four annual magistrates, grouped in two pairs: the *duoviri iure dicundo* for jurisdiction, and two *aediles* for building and finance, though these were sometimes helped by a pair of quaestors. Every sixth year the senior pair, named the *quinquennales*, had to fill up the local senate (*ordo*) and attend to public contracts and the registration of citizens and their property. The magistrates were elected by the townsfolk, who otherwise had little constitutional function and seem to have lost even this electoral power in the second century. The everyday business of the town was conducted in accordance with decrees of the senate whose members, named *decuriones* or *curiales*, usually numbered about 100 and were drawn from the wealthier members of the town, including the former magistrates. They were expected to dip into their own pockets in the public interest, while magistrates helped to provide public games. The more men who could be persuaded to become public benefactors by providing public buildings at their own expense, the better for local taxation. Membership of the *ordo* was at first eagerly sought as an honour, but since it involved increasing expense it ultimately lost its popularity and became a burden to be avoided, if possible. The stone coffin of one councillor found at York and containing a skeleton wearing his official

Wroxeter, *civitas* (tribal capital) of the Cornovii, was embellished in AD 131 by a handsome new forum.

gold ring set with a ruby, is inscribed: 'To the memory of Flavius Bellator, a *decurio* of the *colonia* of Eboracum. He lived for 29 years' (normally the minimum age for office was 30). Another inscription records that a councillor of Gloucester lived to be 80.

The *coloniae* and *municipia* also had colleges of *Augustales*, who maintained the worship of the emperor; their six annual officers, or *seviri*, were elected from the more wealthy freedmen of a town, thus providing a social outlet for this class as well as demonstrating loyalty to the Roman emperor. One such was Marcus Aurelius Lunaris, *sevir Augustalis* of the *coloniae* of York and Lincoln, who dedicated an altar to the goddess Boudig at Bordeaux in fulfilment of a vow he had made when he sailed on business from York. Towns of all sorts had pontiffs and augurs to attend to the ordinary non-imperial cults and religious practices. Thus at Bath (Aquae Sulis) L. Marcius Memor, a *haruspex*, dedicated a statue to the goddess Sulis. A *haruspex* was a diviner who, following old Etruscan practices, inspected the entrails of a sacrificed animal and interpreted the signs which he read there.

The constitutions of the *civitates* no doubt followed the general pattern of those in the *municipia*. The local aristocracy shouldered the civic duties, serving as councillors or senators. For example, inscriptions record a dedication to Hadrian in AD 131 for the building of the forum by the *civitas Cornoviorum*, and from Brough-on-Humber (Petuaria) a few years later a dedication reads: '*Civitas* of the Parisi. For the honour of the divine house of the emperor . . . Antoninus Pius, father of his country, three times consul, and to the deities [*numinibus*] of the emperors, Marcus Ulpius Januarius, *aedile* of the *vicus* of Petuaria, presented this stage [*proscaenium*] at his own expense.' The name Ulpius shows that the emperor Ulpius Traianus had granted Roman citizenship to Januarius' father or grandfather, who had probably served as an auxiliary soldier. His family had apparently then settled down in the civilian zone, where the possession of Roman citizenship would have given them social advantages.

The *civitates* were scattered independent local units, but they and the other towns in the province were bound together by one other bond in addition to the will of the governor, namely the maintenance of the imperial cult. The worship of the emperor flourished throughout the empire, and however much or little it meant in any religious sense, there is no doubt that it gradually came to act as a strong unifying influence both between the various provinces and also within each individual province: like the British Crown in Empire and Commonwealth, it increasingly formed a strong sentimental link of loyalty. It was focused on a provincial council (*concilium provinciae*), which met annually at an altar of the imperial cult. In Britain this was at Colchester, probably in later as well as in earlier times, where an annually elected high priest (*sacerdos*) was responsible for the ceremonies at the temple of Claudius, namely sacrifices, banquets, games and the like. The council might pass votes of thanks or censure on retiring governors, but it had little political power. However, its delegates from the various towns could informally discuss matters of their own interest, and formally speak for the province and even appoint a patron (*patronus provinciae Britanniae*) to represent them in Rome. From the Roman point of view, the *concilium* acted as a useful safety-valve for provincial feelings.

One major administrative change remains to be mentioned: the division of Britain into two provinces by Septimius Severus in AD 197. Britannia Superior in the south was governed by a consular, Britannia Inferior in the north by a man of praetorian rank. The division was caused by the alarming power of the provincial armies shown in the civil wars of the period, and the consequential desire to avoid assigning too many legions to a single governor.

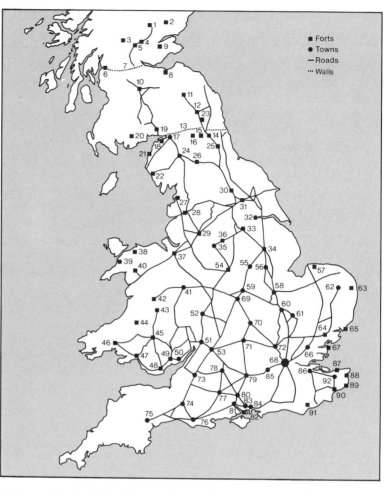

The chief towns, forts and
roads of Roman Britain.
N.B. Some towns started
their lives as forts, but this
development is not shown on
the map.

1 Pinnata Castra (Inchtuthil)
2 (Cardean)
3 (Dalginross)
4 (Strageath)
5 (Ardoch)
6 (Old Kilpatrick)
7 (Antonine Wall)
8 (Inveresk)
9 (Carpow)
10 (Castledykes)
11 Trimontium (Newstead)
12 Bremenium (High
   Rochester)
13 (Hadrian's Wall)
14 Corstopitum (Corbridge)
15 Vercovicium (Housesteads)
16 Vindolanda (Chesterholm)
17 Luguvallium (Carlisle)
18 Maia (Bowness)
19 Blatobulgium (Birrens)
20 (Glenlochar)
21 Alauna (Maryport)
22 Glannaventa (Ravenglass)
23 Habitancum (Risingham)
24 Brocavum (Brougham)
25 Longovicium (Lanchester)
26 Verterae (Brough)
27 (Lancaster)
28 Bremetennacum (Ribchester)
29 Mamucium (Manchester)
30 Isurium (Aldborough)
31 Eboracum (York) colonia
32 Petuaria (Brough)
33 Danum (Doncaster)
34 Lindum (Lincoln) colonia
35 Aquae Arnemetiae
   (Buxton)

36 Navio (Brough, Derbyshire)
37 Deva (Chester)
38 Canovium (Caerhun)
39 Segontium (Caernarvon)
40 (Tomen-y-Mur)
41 Viroconium (Wroxeter)
42 Mediomanum (Caersws)
43 (Castell Collen)
44 (Dolaucothi) mine
45 Cicutio (Y Gaer)
46 Moridunum (Carmarthen)
47 Nidum (Neath)
48 (Cardiff)
49 Isca Silurum (Caerleon)
50 Venta Silurum (Caerwent)
51 Glevum (Gloucester)
   colonia
52 Salinae (Droitwich)
53 Corinium (Cirencester)
54 Derventio (Littlechester)
55 Margidunum (Castle Hill)

56 Causennae (Ancaster)
57 Branodunum (Brancaster)
58 Durobrivae (Water
   Newton)
59 Ratae (Leicester)
60 Durovigutum
   (Godmanchester)
61 Durolipons (Cambridge)
62 Venta Icenorum (Caistor)
63 Gariannonum (Burgh
   Castle)
64 Camulodunum (Colchester)
   colonia
65 (Walton Castle)
66 Caesaromagus (Chelmsford)
67 Othona (Bradwell)
68 Londinium (London)
69 Venonae (High Cross)
70 Lactodorum (Towcester)
71 (Alchester)
72 Verulamium (St Albans)

73 Aquae Sulis (Bath)
74 Lindinis (Ilchester)
75 Isca Dumnoniorum (Exeter)
76 Durnovaria (Dorchester)
77 Sorviodunum (Old Sarum)
78 Cunetio (Mildenhall)
79 Calleva (Silchester)
80 Venta Belgarum
   (Winchester)
81 Clausentum (Bitterne)
82 Portus Adurni (Portchester)
83 (Fishbourne) villa
84 Noviomagus (Chichester)
85 Pontes (Staines)
86 Durobrivae (Rochester)
87 Regulbium (Reculver)
88 Rutupiae (Richborough)
89 Dubris (Dover)
90 Lemanis (Lympne)
91 Anderita (Pevensey)
92 Durovernum (Canterbury)

6

Life in the towns

The units established by Roman charter (*coloniae* and *municipia*), and the native *civitas* capitals, clearly must be classified as towns. But when does a settlement become a town? Although many writers on Roman Britain avoid, perhaps unnecessarily, the word village, many small settlements which in everyday speech we should call villages did exist, and the Latin word *vicus* could be used to describe such a straggling, uncoordinated 'natural' village. But *vicus* is an awkward word since it has a confusing range of meanings. It may refer to 'villages', especially those which grew up outside forts, but it was also applied to some canton capitals, and also even to a specific quarter or ward within a town. Further, *vici* could exist on private or imperial estates, whether they depended on landlord or imperial procurator, while they were distinct from the purely country districts (*pagi*). Clearly small unplanned *vici* arose in a variety of ways, as a result of varied economic and social needs and pressures. Some grew out of native settlements, others from settlements outside military posts. When the soldiers moved on, the settlers might stay behind, while other *vici* remained attached to permanent stations, as at Housesteads on Hadrian's Wall. Others developed around posting-stations on the main roads, where changes of horses and accommodation were made available. Others again might be stimulated by market centres and similar economic needs, while some might have a more specialized origin, such as a shrine like Bath, whose hot waters enabled what was at first perhaps a small cult centre to grow into a prosperous Roman spa.

Towns, large or small, rapidly increased in size and number, and we have already traced their early development until Boudicca's revolt imposed a temporary setback. This, as we have seen, was followed by a great surge forward when the Flavian dynasty was firmly in control at Rome and Agricola implemented the policy of urbanization in Britain itself. It received further impetus from the need to provide more new tribal centres after the death of Cogidubnus, while the campaigns in Wales and Scotland drew troops and garrisons away from the southeast where civilian administration and urbanization could expand. Still further growth resulted from Hadrian's visit in AD 121 or 122. His new policy of creating a permanent frontier in the north involved removing military units from some of the forts in Wales and Brigantia to man the Wall, so that new urban centres of civilian administration had to be established in South Wales and Yorkshire. Furthermore, the emperor's personal presence and interest in the island (not to mention any direct imperial financial help) will have led to new confidence and, as a result, to fresh building activity in the towns. The half century from AD 80 to 130 was the great period of urbanization in Britain.

Although some towns would naturally have outstripped others and developed individual traits, in general the pattern was pretty uniform. Each town had its forum, basilica, temples, baths, shops, private houses and water supply. Urban life flourished, and no protective walls were needed in the peaceful part of the province. The next major change was the almost universal provision of town walls. The dating of this spectacular development has been much debated, but the evidence now points to a gradual process. A very few towns, e.g. St Albans, Winchester and Silchester, seem to have had some defensive earthworks in the first century, but most were fortified only at the end of the second century when some (Silchester, Cirencester, St Albans, Caerwent and Exeter) may even have had masonry gates and towers.

This defensive action may possibly have been taken by Clodius Albinus in order to protect the towns in 196, when he withdrew his troops in his bid for the empire. Later on, fairly early in the third century, the replacement of these earthworks with stone walls was gradually started, and continued for some 50 years. This great building programme meant that by the fourth century all the towns had thick stone walls, backed by earth banks (generally the older earth ramparts), with defensive ditches in front. Although somewhat later than was once thought, the precise dating of these walls is uncertain: possibly Caracalla (211–17) initiated the plan after Severus' campaigns, possibly Alexander Severus (222–35) a little later.

The dating of London's wall is an interesting story. The evidence of a coin of AD 183–4, together with pottery in earlier deposits, shows that it could not have been built before *c.* 190. A *terminus ante quem* is provided by the work of a Roman forger who *c.* AD 220 was turning out silver denarii, for which he used moulds made from genuine coins minted from 201 to 215. For some reason, perhaps to destroy incriminating evidence, he threw away the moulds, together with a denarius of 213–17 and some bronze coins, into some rubbish under a stairway in a tower of the wall. Hence the wall was probably not built until later than *c.* 210.

Before long Saxon raids began to threaten towns on the coast. Rome's response was to build the forts of the Saxon Shore. The process was expensive, and the empire as a whole was going through a desperate period of economic and political upheaval which nearly destroyed it in the mid-third century. Britain on the fringe may have felt some repercussions, and public spending may have been curtailed, but there was no real decline in city life. Though new building may have slackened for a while, existing structures would have sufficed for some time. And unlike the parallel development in Gaul, the area of the towns encircled by the new walls was not reduced; any shrinkage was exceptional. Thus Constantius in 296 not only made good the recent damage done in the north, but also encouraged some building in the south. Confidence returned, and fresh construction was carried out in many towns, large and small, and in the military *vici* in the north.

Much later, when the north suffered further barbarian invasion, and not only the Wall but much of Britain was overrun in 367, Count Theodosius

Left, the walled city of Caerwent (Venta Silurum) as it may have looked at the end of the second century. Though only 44 acres in size, the little town possessed all the standard public buildings and baths. *Above*, a still extant section of the wall, complete with bastion.

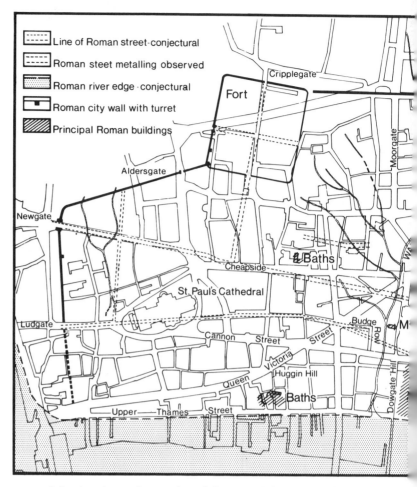

Line of Roman street·conjectural
Roman steet metalling observed
Roman river edge·conjectural
Roman city wall with turret
Principal Roman buildings

Cripplegate

Fort

Moorgate

Aldersgate

Newgate

Baths

Cheapside

St. Paul's Cathedral

Ludgate

Budge Row

Cannon   Street

Victoria Street

Queen

Huggin Hill

Baths

Dowgate Hill

Upper——Thames——Street

restored the situation and strengthened the town defences by adding external towers to the walls, on which artillery could be mounted. This involved filling in the external V-shaped ditch and digging a new one, now U-shaped, a little further beyond the wall where the enemy could be halted within range of the *ballistae*. Garrisons, including trained artillerymen, may have been provided to man the walls. Thus the towns now became strongpoints of defence in a changing world where the barbarians were numerous and threatening, but lacked the skill to storm the walls. In another context the Gothic leader Fritigern reminded his barbarian troops that they were inexperienced in conducting sieges (*ignari obsidiendi*) and that he 'kept peace with the walls' (*pacem sibi esse parietibus*).

The towns continued to prove their worth in the fifth century, when the central government in Rome had to abandon Britain and leave its defence against the barbarians in the islanders' own hands. Protected by their strong walls, they held the Anglo-Saxon raiders at bay for a long time, and offered refuge to the inhabitants of the villages and countryside beyond. Ultimately they succumbed, but they represented a means which the Romans had provided for sustaining independent life well into the period when Rome

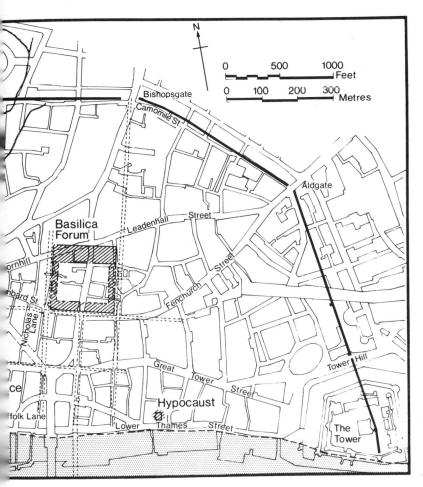

The Roman city of London. Town walls were not added till early in the third century.

itself had been forced to abandon the island to its own fate. The Saxons, even when victorious, had little taste or aptitude for town life. As a result, though pockets of settlement of a sort lingered on in some of the towns, their culture had died, and town life did not return until late Saxon and medieval times.

About the size of the towns we can form fairly clear ideas, but estimates of the population involve a wide range of speculation. In general the towns seem to have been very small, judged by modern standards. The largest were London (330 acres within the walls), Cirencester (240 acres), St Albans (225 acres), and Wroxeter (200 acres). At the other extreme, Gloucester had only 46 acres and Caerwent 44. In between were towns such as Winchester (138) and Canterbury (130), while Colchester and Silchester had about 100 each. But towns did not have walls in early days, and later they might spread beyond them. Therefore some fluctuation beyond the walls must be taken into account. This can be traced at St Albans, where the first-century town covered 119 acres, expanding to 225 in the late second century and contracting to 200 in the fourth century.

Population obviously depends on the density of occupation. Silchester provides an open site within the walls, but we do not know the extent of the

Above, the ghost of Roman Silchester. Crop marks invisible except from the air reveal the outlines of the vanished buildings. *Right*, fourth-century St Albans in plan. The city was divided into blocks (*insulae*) by a grid of streets.

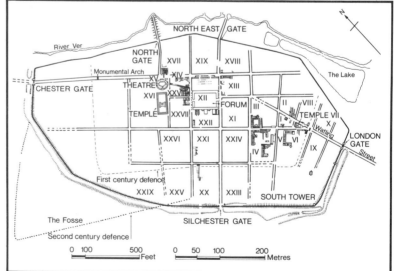

NORTH EAST GATE

River Ver

NORTH GATE

The Lake

Monumental Arch

CHESTER GATE

THEATRE

TEMPLE

FORUM

TEMPLE VII

LONDON GATE

Watling Street

SOUTH TOWER

First century defence

The Fosse

Second century defence

SILCHESTER GATE

XVII XIX XVIII XIV XV XIII XVI XXVIII XII XXVII XXII XI III II VIII X V VI IX IV XXVI XXI XXIV XXIX XXV XX XXIII

0 100 500 Feet

0 50 100 200 Metres

98

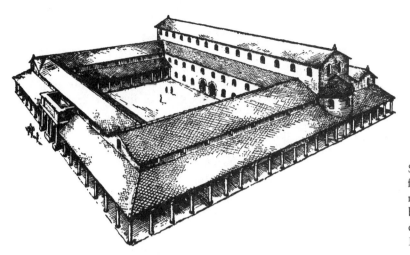

Silchester forum and basilica from the northeast, in reconstruction. Such buildings constituted the centre of all Roman and Romanized cities.

wooden buildings in the ancient built‑up area. However, its amphitheatre could have had some 2,700 seats, and this figure may well correspond roughly with the adult population. Tacitus records that London, St Albans and Colchester lost 70,000 souls when sacked by Boudicca's troops; allowing for some exaggeration, this might indicate a population of *c.* 30,000 for London, and *c.* 15,000 for the other two. But these were exceptionally large, and even Lincoln and Gloucester which, together with some cantonal capitals, might have mustered perhaps 5,000 inhabitants each, were large compared with many other such capitals and lesser towns, which may not have reached more than 2,000 to 3,000, or even less. Such estimates, which are of course very speculative, gain support when compared with the populations of some medieval towns: Winchester near the end of the fourteenth century had 2,100 inhabitants.

THE BUILDINGS

The economic, social and cultural needs of the towns found outward expression in the buildings that adorned them. The streets were laid out on a grid system, dividing the buildings into blocks (*insulae*) which contained public buildings, shops and private houses. The central *insula* was usually occupied by a forum, which formed the civic centre. This was an open rectangular area, with colonnades on three sides and a town hall (*basilica*) on the fourth. The colonnades led to rooms which served as offices and shops. The basilica, which was used as the seat of the law courts, dominated the forum (in many other parts of the Roman empire the dominating building was a temple, the Capitolium, of which there may be traces at St Albans and possibly Colchester).

Two examples of fora may be mentioned. At Silchester the central piazza, measuring 142 feet by 130 feet, was entered through a monumental gate in the east and surrounded on three sides by a portico. The basilica of 233 feet by 58 feet formed the fourth side, with a semicircular tribunal at each end of the nave. The apse in the centre was too small to accommodate the members of the *curia*, and may have been a shrine, though presumably the building did enclose a meeting place for the councillors (*decuriones*). At St Albans the forum was much larger, being 530 feet by 385 feet over all, with a piazza of 310 feet by 205 feet, but this was exceptional in having the *curia* separate from the basilica. It lay in the centre of the opposite side of the forum, and was flanked by small apsed rooms for the *duoviri* and *aediles*. In 1955 fragments were found of an inscription which dates the building to AD 79: it contains part of the name of Agricola. The even larger forum of London has already been described (see p. 55).

The forum was also a trade centre. It generally contained a market hall (*macellum*) where shops could be rented or stalls set up, but sometimes the *macellum* might be a separate building adjacent to the main forum, e.g. at Cirencester, where the discovery of animal bones suggests a meat market. Another public building was the *mansio*, a kind of hotel where officials, including members of the imperial posting service (*cursus publicus*), could lodge. A very large building at Silchester is thought to have been one of these. It was a two-storeyed house built round a courtyard, with an outer courtyard, baths and stables. Another *mansio* was identified very recently at Lower Wanborough (Durocornovium) near Swindon, Wilts., a staging post on the road between Cirencester and Winchester.

In the towns, and indeed outside, were many temples, some of classical design but the majority of the so-called Romano-Celtic type. Examples of the former are found at Colchester and Bath, and it is probable that the imperial cult, though centred at Colchester, had its temples and altars in very many towns. A temple of distinctively Italian style is found at Wroxeter, though the deity to whom it was dedicated remains unknown. The Romano-Celtic type of temple was very different, consisting of a small square central chamber with plastered walls. This rose like a tower above a surrounding, rectangular tiled veranda with a sloping roof, supported by short pillars on a platform. This veranda or portico was either open to the

The *mansio* (roadhouse) at Godmanchester, Cambridgeshire, with public baths at the rear.

The Romano-British temple at Silchester: a reconstruction showing the portico ambulatory surrounding the central shrine.

weather or took the form of an enclosed ambulatory. Many such temples are known, and the remains of their concentric rectangles often show up well in air photography. Several are found at Silchester: at least two, with red-painted stucco walls, were located near the east gate in what appears to have been a religious area, while in another part stood a temple to Mars. Such temples did not receive congregations inside, but rather formed centres at which individuals could offer sacrifice or make their vows, while sacred enclosures around the temples provided space for small gatherings of worshippers.

Next to godliness comes cleanliness, and public baths were a very important feature of the towns, not only for hygiene but also as social centres where citizens could meet, exercise or relax and gossip. Most towns had at least one, many had several of these, and they could be in either public or private ownership. Silchester again provides a good example (see overleaf). The visitor entered through an imposing portico, with adjacent latrines, to a courtyard (*palaestra*) where exercise or sport could be enjoyed. Then on to an undressing-room (*apodyterium*) equipped with clothes-lockers in niches, followed by a plunge in a cold bath (*frigidarium*); then a tepid room

The foundations of a Romano-British temple at Maiden Castle, formerly a Celtic hillfort, reveal the typical concentric arrangement.

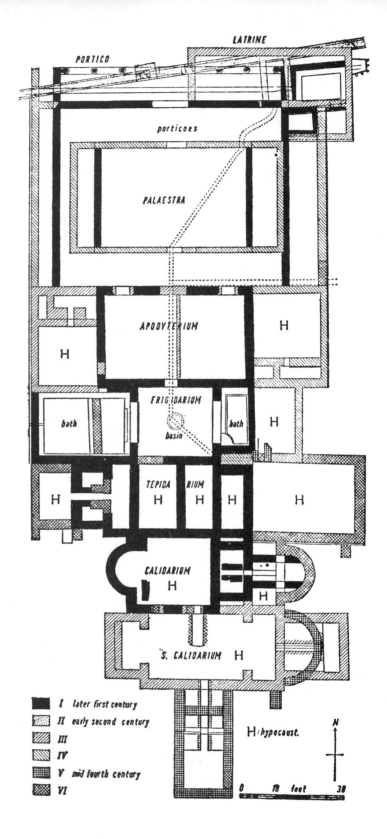

LATRINE

PORTICO

porticoes

PALAESTRA

APODYTERIUM

H

H

FRIGIDARIUM

bath

bath

basin

H

H

TEPIDA RIUM

H

H H H H

H

CALIDARIUM

H

H

S. CALIDARIUM H

I   later first century
II early second century
III
IV
V   mid fourth century
VI

H : hypocaust.

N

0   10 feet   30

Plan of the public baths at
Silchester.

(*tepidarium*), a hot room (*caldarium*) and, if he wanted it, a sweating-hot room (*sudarium*). He scraped himself down with a hook-shaped 'strigil' and might be massaged with oil and perfumes by bath attendants. Finally he could finish off with another cold plunge, if he so wished. But swimming-baths are only found at spas such as Bath or Buxton. The walls of the baths were very thick to conserve the heat, which came from furnaces sending hot air into the area below the floors. These were raised on small pillars (hypocausts), and box-tile flues built into the walls helped to warm the rooms above. It has been calculated that once the floor had been heated up (which might take a day and a half), a room 17 feet by 15 feet could be kept at a temperature of 73 °F by stoking the furnace only twice a day.

A bath-house needed water even more than heat, and this was usually available from local rivers and springs. Again, Silchester provides good examples, while numerous wells afforded domestic supplies. These were 8–30 feet deep, and lined with timber in the lower parts and with flints in the upper. Further water supplies, however, had to be brought in from outside the towns, for the larger bath-houses needed vast supplies which could be obtained only from aqueducts. Varied examples of these are known at Lincoln, Dorchester and Wroxeter. Compared with the great aqueducts that stride on arches across the countryside in Italy, France and Spain, those in Britain are small affairs, yet still important. At Lincoln, for instance, water

The main hot bath at the Roman spa of Bath (Aquae Sulis). Constructed around the famous thermal spring, the city's career as a watering place began with the Romans.

Section of a Roman waterpump.

was brought from a stream called Roaring Meg over a mile away by a pipeline made of earthernware pipes fitting into each other and encased in waterproof concrete.

Roman engineers knew how to construct hydraulic free-pumps, as the survival of one at Silchester indicates. At Dorchester an open unlined channel, some five feet wide at the bottom, was skilfully constructed from the river Frome for a distance of 11 miles to the town where it is reckoned to have discharged about 13,000,000 gallons of water a day; parts are still visible as an embanked shelf on the hillside. At Wroxeter a similar system delivered approximately 2,000,000 gallons of water a day to a distribution tank. Neither this nor any other such tanks (*castella*) survive in any British towns, but some have been found in military sites in the north, e.g. at Benwell on the Wall. However, considerable traces still exist of the distribution system within Wroxeter, for both public and private users. These consist of both timber and lead pipes running along a street edge; they must have been fed from a main pipe, from which they could be isolated if necessary by means of a sluice-gate. Thus the local authorities could regulate supplies or even cut them off from any private householders who failed to pay their water rates. In Silchester a pipeline has been traced for some 700 feet.

Water had to be brought into the towns, but surplus water also had to be drained off: hence elaborate drainage and sewerage systems. These are best seen at Lincoln, which had large stone-built sewers under all the main streets, with smaller pipes draining into them from private houses and with manholes at intervals. Sewers also drained the public latrines: at St Albans, for example, a main sewer ran down from the forum to the river and collected waste from a latrine *en route*. Smaller towns may have had less elaborate systems, but at Chichester two large sewers, one timber-lined, have been found, while at Caistor-by-Norwich air photography has revealed a number of dark lines running down the centre of the streets, and these were probably sewers. The Romans were expert engineers, not least in controlling water, and it was a governor of Britain, Frontinus, who wrote the standard work 'On Aqueducts', and served in Rome as *curator aquarum* in AD 97.

For entertainment many towns had theatres or amphitheatres, or both. Theatres are known only at Canterbury, St Albans, Colchester and Brough. One, not yet identified, is mentioned by Tacitus as being within the early town of Colchester, while a second lay outside the town at Gosbecks Farm. That at Brough (Petuaria) is also unknown, but is attested by an inscription which, as we have seen (p. 90), records that Januarius, a local aedile, presented the stage in honour of the emperor Antoninus Pius. The little theatre at Gosbecks Farm and the one at Canterbury, which was built *c.* AD 80–90, perhaps originally with timber seats on banks of gravel, are Romano-British adaptations of the usual classical D-shaped form. This consisted of a semicircular area (*orchestra*) surrounded by tiers of seats (*cavea*) facing a rectangular stage. The well-preserved theatre at St Albans, built soon after a widespread fire had damaged much of the town *c.* AD 155 (though it may have had a predecessor), possessed a more nearly circular *orchestra*. When it was enlarged in the fourth century it followed the classical model more closely, as did the Canterbury theatre when it was rebuilt early in the third

Above, the Roman theatre of
St Albans (Verulamium),
the best preserved in Britain,
was built on the site of a
previous theatre destroyed in
the fire of 155. *Left*, the
theatre as it may have
appeared when in use.

century. The seating capacity of the theatres seems to have been large in relation to the population of the towns: that at Canterbury could hold an audience of some 7,000.

The shows would consist of plays, pantomimes, singing or recitations, no doubt of varying degrees of sophistication or vulgarity. It is noteworthy, however, that elsewhere in the Roman empire theatres are often found near temples or shrines, as indeed they are at St Albans and Gosbecks Farm. They may, therefore, also have been used for large religious gatherings and perhaps religious performances. The actors in classical plays wore masks; some of these, made of ivory or clay, have survived at Caerleon, Catterick and Baldock, and others are illustrated in second-century paintings at Leicester.

More violent forms of Roman entertainment were chariot-racing in the circus, and gladiatorial contests and animal fights in the amphitheatre. No trace of any circuses has yet been found in Roman Britain, but since both the natives and the Romans were fond of hunting, some form of horse-racing, if

not chariot-racing, may often have been organized. However, a tombstone from Old Penrith depicts a boy holding a palm branch and (apparently) a whip, and he might have been the victor in a boys' chariot-race. A sculpture from Lincoln shows a boy driving a chariot, while a mosaic in a Lincolnshire country house actually illustrates a chariot-race – but it must be remembered that mosaic scenes were often stereotyped and may not always reflect scenes of local contemporary life.

Amphitheatres on the other hand were widespread. They consisted of an oval arena, completely surrounded by rising tiers of seats which had gaps for entrances; the Colosseum at Rome is the outstanding exemplar. Those in Britain mostly had earth banks on which timber seats were fixed, though a few were stone-built. They were generally on the outskirts of the towns, and when these were surrounded by walls the amphitheatres were left outside. The best-preserved example is at Caerleon, where the amphitheatre was attached to the fortress of the Second Legion and was presumably used as a

Chariot-racing, here depicted on a mosaic from a villa at Horkstow, Lincs., probably represents one kind of entertainment to be found in Roman Britain.

Above, the amphitheatre at
Caerleon, constructed
c. AD 80, may have been
used primarily for military
training. Entertainments
included gladiatorial contests,
as on the 'gladiator vase' from
Colchester (*right*), where the
combatants are named as
Memnon and Valentinus.

A jet bear from Colchester illustrates the type of animal found in, and exported from, Roman Britain.

parade-ground for military training as well as for amusement. The arena measured 184 feet by $136\frac{1}{2}$ feet, and was surrounded by a 12-foot wall to protect the 6,000 or so spectators. It was built *c.* AD 80 by the legionaries, and an inscription records the work of one unit: 'From the tenth cohort, the century of Flavius Julinus [built this]'.

Another legionary amphitheatre, at Chester, was built in wood by Legio II Adiutrix *c.* AD 78 and was replaced in stone on a larger scale when Legio XX came to the fortress. In the civilian town established at Caerwent, near Caerleon, an amphitheatre seems to have been built in the late third or fourth century over some earlier houses and within the city walls (alternatively the building has been identified as a large livestock market). Other examples are found at Silchester (not yet excavated), Dorchester (now grass-covered and built, perhaps in the late first century, around the Neolithic monument of Maumbury Rings half a mile south of the town), Chichester and Cirencester (both also late first century), Carmarthen in South Wales, and even outside an auxiliary fort at the wild mountain site at Tomen-y-Mur in North Wales. The principal purpose of the latter is likely to have been military rather than recreational. The amphitheatre at York is known only by implication: a carving shows a gladiator [*retiarius*] with net and trident, while a plaque is inscribed '*Domine victor vinces felix*', a phrase often used about gladiators. At Leicester both a gladiator and an actress are commemorated, their names being carefully scratched on a piece of pottery: 'Verecunda the actress [*ludia*], Lucius the gladiator.'

Of the nature of gladiatorial combats and beast-hunts (*venationes*) little can be said here. Clearly they would have been on a small scale compared with those in the richer provinces of the Roman empire, and would have varied according to the wealth of individual cities and of the local magistrates who were responsible for them. The arenas and amphitheatres probably witnessed more baiting of bulls or bears than lions or elephants. However lions, and a bear, appear on fragments of pottery from Colchester; a brooch from Lakenheath appears to depict a man fighting a lion. Bears, which may also have been trained to perform, were found in Britain, and indeed were even

A large courtyard house at Silchester, in reconstruction. The house stood on an angle of the street grid, and the garden is thought to have contained flowers and herbs.

exported: the poet Martial records the appearance of a Caledonian bear in the arena at Rome in the reign of Domitian (sent by Agricola?). Gladiatorial shows are depicted on a mosaic in a villa at Bignor (Sussex), with cupids acting as gladiators, and a gladiatorial bronze helmet has been found at Bury St Edmunds; statuettes of gladiators come from London and South Shields, and they are also depicted on vases – eight appear on a green glass cup from Colchester. However it must be remembered that scenes on imported objects (or indeed on locally made mosaics) may reflect the interests of the owner, and not necessarily contemporary events.

The shops and houses in towns are not always easy to distinguish from each other, since the same building often served both as home and business premises. A normal form of shop consisted of a narrow strip with its long axis at right angles to the street on to which it opened. Many were constructed of clay on a timber framework, sometimes with a stone foundation. The front, which faced the street, might be largely open, possibly with wooden shutters, and serving as both shop and workroom. The family lived in rooms at the rear, or sometimes possibly on an upper storey – but the evidence for this is uncertain, and in any case the upper floor may have been used as a storage loft rather than as living quarters. Houses of such simple materials continued to be built well into the second century, *c.* AD 130 at London and *c.* 155 at St Albans, when solider buildings were erected following fire damage. Some larger buildings, of course, already existed (examples are found at St Albans and Wroxeter), and these might be L-shaped or built round a courtyard. The better ones gradually acquired concrete floors, hypocausts in place of braziers, mosaics and painted walls, with translucent (but not transparent) glass windows. Some mosaic work appears at Canterbury in the first century, but not much before 150 at St Albans; at Cirencester painted wall-plaster is found as early as the Flavian period, and stone, which was available locally, began to replace timber-framing not much later.

The shops might be owned by their inhabitants, or run by tenant freedmen or slave managers. In one block (*Insula* xiv) at St Albans, both the original Claudian buildings and those rebuilt after Boudicca's destruction were in single ownership, built by a local landowner and let out as individual premises to tenants. After further rebuildings around the mid-second century they were gradually broken up into individual blocks, just as soon, no doubt, as each tenant began to prosper and acquire his own premises. Also at this period large and even luxurious private houses appear in the towns. At Cirencester it is possible to trace how some premises in a row of timber-built shops were gradually replaced in stone as each shopkeeper could afford this improvement, until by the fourth century the whole row had been converted into stone.

While the overall pattern of the towns may have been similar, each would naturally have developed its own individuality, but unfortunately their separate histories cannot be followed here.

Outside the towns lay the cemeteries, for Roman law did not allow burials within cities, and most urban cemeteries were to be found lining the roads leading out. Both cremation and inhumation were practised in pre-Roman, as in Roman, Britain, while in the Roman empire at large the former tended to give place to the latter from the later second century AD. In Britain, round tumuli had covered the remains of the rich and powerful as far back as the Bronze Age. Later Belgic barrows of the Iron Age are exemplified by two found at Lexden near Colchester. the majority contained cremations, but there were a few inhumations.

Cremations in Roman Britain were marked by tombstones for individuals or families, where these could be afforded, or by an earth mound; masonry tombs and columbaria were also built. The remains of the poor were covered with tiles or stones. Later, with the increase of inhumation, sarcophagi and coffins were employed, the body sometimes being embalmed in gypsum, and in Christian cemeteries – as at Poundbury at Dorchester – the inhumations were generally orientated east and west. The objects buried with the dead naturally varied in accordance with the wealth or poverty of the individual, so that outside most towns one might expect to find a variety of funeral monuments. Walled cemeteries were more normal in the countryside, especially in southeast Britain.

Several cemeteries are known at York. In one of the poorer ones (at Trentholme Drive), about 350 bodies were found dating to *c.* AD 150–400: some 50 per cent of the deaths are reckoned to have occurred between the ages of 20 and 40, and 15 per cent before the age of 20, with only a small proportion surviving after 45. The average height of the men was 5 ft 7 in. (1.699m.), of the women 5 ft 1 in. (1.549m.). The racial origin of the women appears to have been less mixed than that of the men, some of whom may have come from as far as the Eastern Mediterranean. Surprisingly, the inscribed tombstones at York, which represent a higher social status, do not suggest a higher expectation of life.

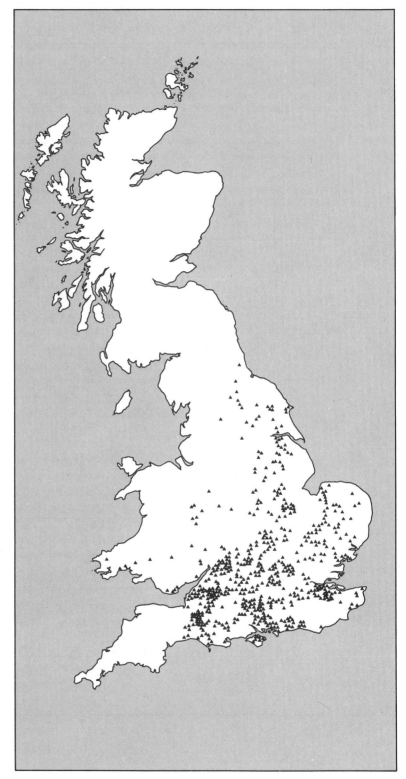

Distribution of villas through
Roman Britain.

7

Villas and countryside

Villas were an outstanding feature of country life in Roman Britain in certain areas and at certain periods. Typically they were large, well-built country houses, with several rooms opening off a long corridor, with hypocausts, tessellated pavements or mosaics, and with projecting wings which formed an open or enclosed courtyard. However, these elaborate farmhouses are only the final culmination in the third and fourth centuries of a long period of development.

In Latin *villa* simply means a farm, though one of a certain size, since other words were used for small units, such as *casa* for cottage. Thus a villa was often the main central building of an estate which might contain cottages and other farm buildings. The word is sometimes used by modern writers only if the occupier had reached a certain standard of civilization, as shown by the architecture and contents of the house. The villa may have been farmed by the owner and his family, partly perhaps with the help of slaves, and with some areas possibly let out to tenants (*coloni*). On the other hand, it need not have been the chief home of its owner, who often lived in a town and perhaps came to the country for a holiday: in that case it would be run by a bailiff and slaves. The practice of exposing unwanted slave children is suggested by the skeletons of 97 infants in the yard of a villa at Hambledon, Bucks. The main point of distinction, however, is that a villa represented a separate unit, and was not an intimate part of another community such as a village. It is better, perhaps, not to be too concerned with the problem, 'When is a villa not a villa?' but rather to try to trace the growth of country settlement from pre-Roman times to the great estates of the fourth century.

The pre-Romans lived, as we have seen (p. 12) in peasant settlements like that at Little Woodbury, with circular huts, storage pits and cultivated 'Celtic' fields. As time went on, rectangular cottages sometimes replaced the round huts, and gradually the inhabitants made greater use of imported Roman pottery and coinage, but the old system continued long into the Roman period. Besides isolated farmsteads, some settlements began to coalesce into hamlets or villages. But the sharp contrast which R. G. Collingwood drew between native villages of small huts and single farmsteads, which he called villas, assuming that some regions were exclusively occupied by villas and others by villages, has now been abandoned. Native settlements, it seems, were more numerous and more interlocked with the villas than was once thought. In the highland zone the inhabitants, still predominantly pastoralists, maintained their more primitive Iron Age conditions, and villa life was excluded.

The gradual improvements and growth under Roman influence are well illustrated by the history of the 'villas' at Lockleys near Welwyn, and at Park Street near St Albans. At Lockleys two pre-Claudian Belgic huts reveal that Roman pottery had superseded Belgic by late Neronian times (*c.* AD 65), and a new rectangular house with five rooms and a veranda was built. The lower walls were stone-built (flints and mortar), the upper probably timber-framed, with painted wall-plaster. This development marked an increase in wealth and comfort, while the subdivision into rooms indicated greater social differentiation between farmer and labourers. Houses of this sort were, of course, not usually occupied by 'Romans' but by British farmers, who probably had turned for their models to the houses in the towns. The Lockleys house was enlarged in the second half of the second century with wings and a corridor, which replaced the veranda. In the earlier house, access

The Lockleys villa, Welwyn, Herts. *Above*, a reconstruction of the villa in its final form; *below*, a plan showing the stages of the villa's development.

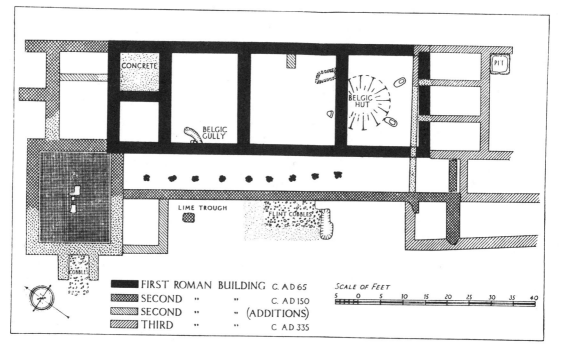

to the rooms was mainly through one to the next, but now a corridor gave separate entrances. A century or more later it was destroyed by fire, but was rebuilt fairly soon, c. 330–40. A similar development at Park Street again shows how, over the centuries, a Belgic hut became a Roman villa.

Naturally the growth of the villas went on at different paces in different places, as wealth and demand increased, but in general few had baths before the later second century, while mosaics came even later, though villas at Angmering and Eccles had them in the first century. Villa life flourished in the period 150–200 partly because the towns newly created by Rome brought into being fresh markets for agricultural produce. After a period of decline it revived, and in the late third and fourth centuries enjoyed even greater prosperity.

The architectural types of villas did not evolve from one another in a neat chronological sequence. We find, for instance, the earliest first-century-type house still being built in the fourth century. Hence it is better to look at the types in relation to their economic background rather than to seek to establish a pattern of development. Archaeologists trace four main groups: the cottage, the winged corridor, the courtyard and the aisled villa.

The simple cottage house, typified, as we have seen, by remains at Lockleys and Park Street, could easily be extended when the need was felt to expand, or further to separate the main family from the rest of the household. A corridor or veranda was built along the front, while projecting rooms were put on at each end. Such was the essential structure of the winged corridor house, although naturally a great variety of detailed plans and additions were devised. It became the normal form of small country house from c. AD 100. Similar buildings are found in France, with an ultimately Italian ancestry,

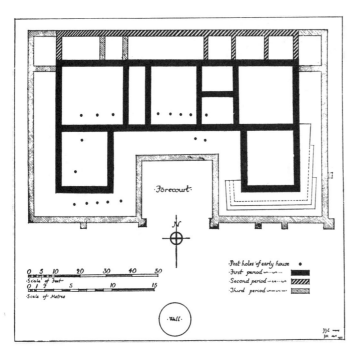

Plan of the villa at Ditchley, Oxon. The so-called winged corridor house was very common during the second century.

while in England there is a good example at Great Staughton in Huntingdonshire, and a slightly more elaborate and comfortable house at Ditchley. In general, however, these corridor houses remained fairly modest and did not form the homestead of the really large estates.

The third type of villa is the courtyard house, which was used for the largest and richest villas. All villas tended to have a space for the farmyard in front, and perhaps various small buildings at the sides. Sometimes two L-shaped groups of buildings were so constructed as to form a kind of courtyard. The typical 'courtyard house', however, had an enclosed rectangular court, generally entered by a front gateway. The main difference between the British examples and their Italian prototypes is that in Britain the courtyard led up to the main house, while the classical form had a garden court within or behind the house. A fine example is at North Leigh in Oxfordshire, where a corridored court, about 200 feet by 160 feet, was surrounded by the wings of the house. The complicated story of this villa's growth may be traced from the small original house occupying the middle position at the back, and accompanied by a little, detached barn-house.

Plan of the villa at North Leigh, Oxon. Built round a rectangular courtyard, this type of villa represented the peak of Romano-British affluence. In the plan *H* stands for hypocaust, *M* for mosaic pavement, and *T* for tessellated floor.

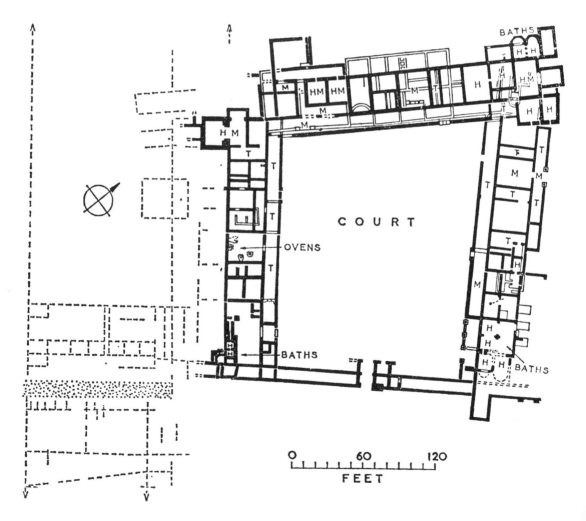

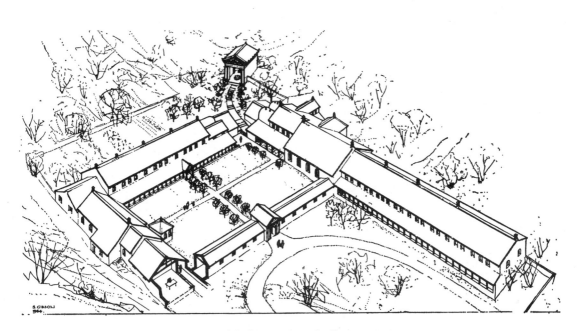

Chedworth in the Cotswolds is one of the best-preserved villas in Britain. The layout which can be seen today belongs to the fourth century, but occupation continued from the first half of the second century until the end of the fourth. The villa had an inner courtyard which was also in part a garden, while an extension of the wings formed a second courtyard. In the fourth century all the buildings were linked by corridors, and a large dining-room and two sets of baths, hot and cold, were built.

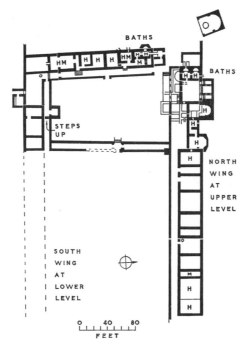

BATHS

BATHS

STEPS
UP

NORTH
WING
AT
UPPER
LEVEL

SOUTH
WING
AT
LOWER
LEVEL

0   40   80
FEET

Chedworth villa in the Cotswolds near Cirencester, perhaps the most scenically sited in Britain, was also one of the richest. *Above*, the villa in reconstruction; *left*, a plan of the building (*H* for hypocaust, *M* for mosaic) reveals its extent.

Llantwit Major, Glamorgan: reconstruction of the villa and farmyard. Despite its westerly location, this was a prosperous villa which was later worked as a farm in the absence of its owners, who left the big house untenanted.

The fourth type, the aisled house (or basilican villa) was a rectangular building. Two rows of pillars ran down the long axis, dividing it into three sections, a nave and two aisles, and supporting the roof. This hall-like structure normally had its entrance in the middle of one side; partitions could be set up inside to create separate rooms if desired. This house was obviously much simpler than the corridor or courtyard types. In some cases it might be little more than a barn adjacent to the main house. It could have served as a separate dwelling for the workers of a richer master, or have sheltered the farmer, his family and perhaps his livestock. A simple example is found at Spoonley Wood in Gloucestershire, but the farm at Clanville near Andover in Hampshire is much more elaborate, with many rooms, tessellated pavements, a mosaic, window glass, painted wall-plaster and a bath. At Llantwit Major in Glamorgan an aisled house coexisted with a courtyard villa and continued to be used after the large house was abandoned by the owner, who presumably had become an absentee landlord living in a town. Though some early examples are found, aisled houses tend to be of a later period.

Villas had out-buildings, which might include an aisled house, for use as barns, cottages and stables. Bath-houses were often separate from the main building, in order to reduce the risk of fire. Threshing-floors must have been common, and many villas had kilns for corn-drying: a furnace flue supplied a gentle heat to a space between two floors above, on the upper of which the corn rested.

Most villas fit into one of the four main categories, but two of exceptional interest deserve special mention: Fishbourne, just west of Chichester in Sussex, and Lullingstone in Kent. Fishbourne is by far the most splendid of the early country mansions. It covered more than five acres and may have served as a palace for Cogidubnus (see p. 50). If not, its owner must have been an important Roman official or an immensely rich Briton. It can be classed as a winged corridor house, but its inspiration was more directly Italian. It superseded a timber military construction *c*. AD 75, and a stone-built house arose on a platform of clay and stones over two acres in extent. The main colonnaded courtyard was some 200 feet square, and the higher dominating west wing was approached by a flight of steps from the main court. These led to a central room which may well have served as an audience chamber. The east wing contained the entrance hall, bath-house, and two peristyle courts. The walls were decorated with marble from Italy and Greece, the floors with black and white mosaics, while the garden was landscaped with paths, hedges and fountains. Despite much rebuilding, the original grandeur was not maintained, and occupation seems to have ended about AD 270.

The villa at Lullingstone, on an embankment overlooking the river Darenth, is noteworthy for its impressive dining-room and a comparative

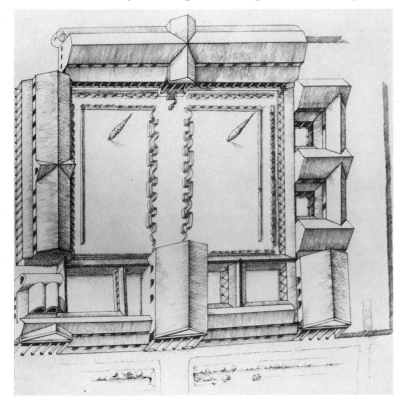

The palace of Fishbourne, near Chichester, is thought to be the seat of Cogidubnus, the Romanized British king of the first century. The reconstruction is in the form of an isometric drawing.

Lullingstone, Kent: a reconstruction of the villa as it appeared in the fourth century, with temple mausoleum.

shortage of other rooms, which suggests that it may have been designed primarily for pleasure rather than as the pivot of an agricultural estate. Its owner may have been non-British, since it contained two sculptured busts in the Eastern Mediterranean style, which may have been family portraits. For much of the third century the villa was neglected: possibly its owner had supported Clodius Albinus and in consequence the estate had been confiscated by the Roman government. However, it was rebuilt more than once in the fourth century, when it had agricultural connections. Its mosaics were exceptionally fine: one depicted Bellerophon, Pegasus and the Chimera, another Europa and the bull, with two lines alluding to Virgil's *Aeneid*. These suggest a cultured pagan owner, but in *c.* 350 a corner was converted into a small Christian chapel (see p. 167) which was decorated with paintings of the Chi-Rho monogram, and of worshippers with outstretched arms (*orantes*). This continued in use until the villa was destroyed by fire in about AD 500.

The histories of individual villas naturally varied, but the general trend seems to have been that a period of great activity occurred at the end of the third century and during the fourth, whether or not there had been something of a recession earlier. Now older farms were rebuilt, new ones

The mosaics of Lullingstone reflect its cultivated owners' classical pagan and Christian interests. *Left*, the famous mosaic of Europa and the bull; *below*, Christian worshippers in beaded robes with their arms outstretched (*orantes*) in a formal gesture of prayer.

A banqueting scene:
fragment from a tombstone
found at Kirkby Thore,
Northumberland.

constructed, and many others became much more luxurious. An interesting
theory, though unsupported by direct evidence, is that the impetus behind
this boom may partly have been due to contemporary barbarian attacks in the
Rhineland and France. Britain by contrast must have seemed a relatively safe
refuge, attracting settlers and their money over the Channel and into the
island. Previously, moreover, farms owned by rich town-dwellers were often
occupied by bailiffs or middle-class farmers, but in the fourth century more of
the aristocratic owners appear to have become directly involved, and perhaps
actually resided, in their country estates for longer periods. Nevertheless the
really rich houses of course remained in the minority, being reckoned at some
75 out of more than 600 known villas. In size, too, the villas must have varied
enormously. The estate of the relatively modest villa at Ditchley has been
calculated at about 1,000 acres in the fourth century, while that at Bignor
may have had 2,000 acres of arable land as well as extensive pasturage, and a
few may even have doubled that figure.

Villas, then, ranged from the luxurious mansion to the small working
farmhouse. Even so, if they are defined as Romanized farms it seems that they
were essentially limited to the lowland zone of Britain, where they were most
numerous in the south. With few exceptions, such as fourth-century
buildings near Durham and the East Riding of Yorkshire, they are not found
in the neighbourhood of Hadrian's Wall or further north, in the greater part
of Wales, in Cornwall, or in Devon west of the river Exe. The distribution of
the villas within the lowland area is uneven, with the lighter chalk uplands
often left to the older peasant settlements, and the villas concentrated on the

richer, heavier soils: thus in Sussex the villas are found north and south of the South Downs, which remained the home of the earlier settlers. But one factor was dominant in the choice of sites: their distance from towns. Villas were working farms and, therefore, had to be in contact with their markets, so that their viability depended on their access to roads and towns.

However, the noticeable absence of villas from two large areas, Wessex and the Fenland, requires further comment. In some 900 square miles round Salisbury Plain and Cranbourne Chase peasant farmsteads and villages abound, but there are hardly any villas. In the Fen Basin, flooding prevented practically all Iron Age settlement, but in the first century AD occupation was made possible by slight changes in the sea-land level. Man then intervened and drainage was undertaken, but this was on such a large scale as to suggest official action. The Roman government may well have taken over and developed this area as imperial property. Prasutagus left Nero part of his kingdom by will, and after the revolt of the Iceni the Romans very likely seized more. This theory gains credence from the absence of private villas. After extensive drainage works, starting perhaps *c.* AD 80, the reclaimed land was settled by peasants who were provided with farms for which they paid rent. Further development probably followed Hadrian's visit to Britain. There is no trace here of centuriation, a method of dividing the land into rectangular plots, that was normally used by the Romans when distributing land officially. The farms, which may have been grouped in small family villages, produced sheep, cattle and salt, as well as grain. The area was seriously flooded early in the third century, but regained something of its old prosperity by the end. This lasted only as long as the drainage system was maintained, and it probably lapsed even before the end of Roman rule at the beginning of the fifth century.

The absence of villas in the Wessex area may also have been due to its annexation as an imperial estate, perhaps as punishment for the powerful resistance that the locals had originally offered to the Roman invaders. A further consideration that points to imperial control, both here and in the Fenland, is the proximity of both to military areas during the early period. Wessex was well placed for supplying corn across the Bristol Channel to the Roman army at Caerleon, and the Fenland could help to feed the troops at York, by means of some intermediate canals such as the Car Dyke and other waterways. While the Fenland continued to send corn to the north of England, and probably also to export some to the armies in the Rhineland (especially in the fourth century), Wessex later began to turn to stock-breeding, particularly sheep. Corn on the imperial estates was presumably grown by natives to whom the government had granted tenancies. In early days the Britons had to hand over grain as a corn tax (*annona*) and pay for its transport. It is possible that later this levy was relaxed (by Hadrian?) except in wartime, in which case the natives would have sold the grain to the authorities at the market price. But if the *annona* continued, it was probably collected more equitably than in the early days of conquest when the abuses of the procurators, denounced by Tacitus, seem confirmed by the discovery of an official corn measure, capable of holding more corn than indicated by the figure inscribed on the outside of the vessel.

8

Economic life

AGRICULTURE

Agriculture, the basis of Celtic life in Britain, remained the fundamental industry in Roman times. The Romans no doubt transformed the whole country with their policy of urbanization, but the life of the towns themselves depended on the farmers. The Romans also changed the pattern of settlement in the country itself by stimulating the development of a new unit of production, the villa, and by greatly extending the area of farmland. But in the countryside old ways and practices long continued, and technical advances, though far from negligible, were less spectacular than might have been expected.

Evidence from villas and towns shows gradual improvements in tools and implements such as hammers, saws, axes, planes and the like, while the introduction of a two-handed scythe for hay-cutting, together with a balanced sickle, rakes, and iron-shod spades, made work easier. A reaping-machine (*vallus*) was used in Gaul and may have been brought into Britain. Storage pits gradually disappeared in favour of granaries and barns, and corn-drying methods improved. Geared wheels helped to harness animal- or water-power to mills, and Roman skills enabled deeper wells to be dug. The history of the plough remains controversial. Even in Belgic times the native plough had been improved, and later a heavier iron-bar share and a coulter, which cut the soil ahead of the share, were introduced, besides a mould-board, which could turn a furrow to one side or the other. Whatever the details, the effect was that heavier soils could now be exploited, though poorer farmers might well have had to remain content with the earlier simpler plough.

Most farming was mixed, combining both arable and pasture, and crops were improved. Spelt, the staple product, was supplemented with rye, oats and flax. Many new vegetables, such as cabbages, peas, parsnips, turnips and carrots, were introduced, together with new varieties of fruit – plums, apples, cherries and walnuts. The vine appears to have been cultivated at Gloucester and Boxmoor, but the climate precluded its widespread success. Pastoral farming also improved, with the introduction of a better breed of cattle and perhaps also of horses. Pigs and dogs continued to be raised, and bee-keeping was probably commonly practised. Diocletian's Edict of Prices contains a reference to the products of goats and sheep: the *birrus Britannicus*, a hooded cloak of goat's hair, and the *tapete Britannicum*, a wool rug or blanket. At Woodcuts in Wessex thousands of animal bones were discovered, including oxen (40 per cent), sheep (29 per cent), pig (13 per cent), and horses (10 per cent). Dog bones made up much of the rest. On the subject of smaller farm

Opposite, Romano-British opulence: the magnificent fourth-century silver dish, almost two feet across, found at Mildenhall, Suffolk. Imported from the Mediterranean, it depicts Oceanus surrounded by nymphs.

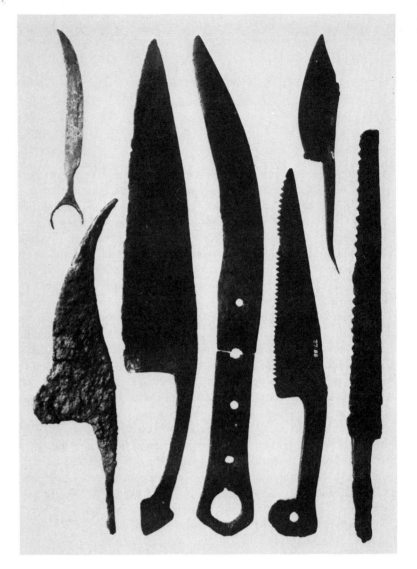

Agriculture in Roman Britain: a selection of iron implements, knives and saws.

animals Caesar makes the curious comment that the Britons kept chickens, geese and hares for amusement, not food (can he have misunderstood some ritual connection?), but such restraint is unlikely to have been maintained in Roman times. Of less practical value was the introduction of the cat, and of flowers such as the rose, lily, violet, pansy and poppy.

Other economic pursuits of the countryside included fishing in rivers and on the coast; shellfish, especially oysters, were also gathered. Hunting, as we have seen, was a widely popular sport: not only were wolves and foxes kept down, but also boars and deer were provided for the larder. Hunting dogs, recorded by Strabo as British exports in Augustus' day, continued in use, and are mentioned by third- and fourth-century writers such as Oppian, Nemesianus, Claudian and Symmachus. They include Irish wolfhounds,

The Romano-British dog: *above*, a bronze (votive?) figurine found near the sanctuary of Nodens at Lydney, Glos. *Left*, a coursing scene on a locally produced Castor ware jar probably reflects native sporting activities.

greyhounds, and a dog used for bull-baiting (perhaps a bulldog?). Caledonian bears were exported to the arena at Rome, as previously noted.

Agriculture was already flourishing in southeast England when Caesar arrived in 55 BC and noted that 'there is an extremely dense population, the [farm]houses are very concentrated in distribution and the cattle are numerous.' These houses would have been small family farmsteads, like the one at Little Woodbury, devoted to growing cereals and raising stock. The island must have been essentially self-sufficient, and agriculture continued to expand, since 50 years or so later under Augustus Britain was exporting corn and cattle in return for 'luxury' goods from Roman Gaul. After the conquest the number of mouths to be fed in Britain increased rapidly, for the Roman army of conquest, and later of occupation, needed food and supplies such as corn, meat and leather.

One issue which has not yet been stressed is the settlement of army veterans in the three *coloniae* founded in the first century. The system commonly practised in Italy and Mediterranean lands, whereby the farmer lived in the town and went out each day to his allotment in the adjacent *territorium*, would presumably have been followed in Britain. The example of the veterans may well have stimulated the cultivation of land around other towns, including tribal *civitates*, and there was a tendency to develop agriculture near the *vici* of the forts. The scarcity of villas around Canterbury, Silchester or London may indicate that the land in the vicinity of these towns was cultivated by the inhabitants themselves. At any rate, the area of cultivation obviously increased, not least with the development of imperial estates and the drainage of the Fenland.

Unfortunately we cannot trace any rise or fall in the native population, nor what proportion of its products went in tax or sale to the authorities. We can see little beyond the general picture of an apparent increasing prosperity, though there may have been ups and downs. As town life expanded, it provided more markets for the country, while the history of the villas shows no very serious recession in the third century and greater prosperity in the fourth. There is regrettably little to be inferred from odd scraps of information such that, during an emergency in AD 359, the emperor Julian was able to increase the export of corn from Britain to the Rhineland to 600 barge-loads, but the absence in Britain of the kind of peasant revolts which afflicted Gaul in the third and fourth centuries suggests continuing prosperity.

METALS

Caesar, as we have seen, mentions bronze, tin, gold and iron in relation to Britain. Such inadequate notions as he held about the mineral wealth of the island may or may not have strengthened his desire to invade it, but contemporary opinion apparently did not rank its resources very high: Cicero in May 54 BC wrote to a young friend named Trebatius, whom he had commended to Caesar, telling him not to be too avaricious since 'I hear that there is not a scrap of gold or silver in Britain.' He adds in jest that Trebatius' best hope would be to capture a British war-chariot. Claudius later may have

Main mining areas and products.

The gold mine at Dolaucothi, Dyfed, was drained by large wooden water-wheels of the type illustrated here.

been tempted by hopes of Britain's wealth, though this implication need not necessarily be read into Tacitus' remark that it produced gold, silver and other metals which are 'the prize of victory' (*pretium victoriae*).

Tin, which Caesar mistakenly attributed to the interior of Britain, had been mined in Cornwall from prehistoric times, but this trade had been disrupted by Caesar's campaigns in Brittany, and Strabo does not mention the metal among the island's exports. By Flavian times Rome drew all the tin she needed from Spain, but when the mines there and in Dacia (Romania) were closed, the British source was opened up again in the mid-third century. Hoards of Roman coins have been found in Cornwall, while tin and pewter vessels occur there and elsewhere (e.g. eight pewter blocks were found in the Thames at Battersea).

If the Romans expected great things of the gold reported in Britain they may have been disappointed. Only one gold mine is known, that at Dolaucothi in southwest Wales (Carmarthenshire). Perhaps they were misled by gold objects which reached Britain from Ireland. However, later Roman mining at Dolaucothi was impressive. The gold-bearing pyrites was extracted by means of open-cast workings and also by underground galleries (145 feet deep at one place) which were drained by large wooden water-wheels, traces of which have been found. Three open-channel aqueducts on the hillside, one of them seven miles long, brought some 3,000,000 gallons of water a day to a main reservoir tank, from which it flowed down a row of stepped washing tables in order to clean the ore after this had been crushed and milled. Water was also used to help break down the softer beds of rock. A building which was once thought to contain pit-head baths, such as existed at Spanish mines, is now generally regarded as belonging to the neighbouring fort at Pumpsaint village. The mines were imperial property, but were probably leased to contractors (*conductores*). A hoard of jewellery – armlets and necklaces – suggests that goldsmiths may have worked on the spot.

Silver was extracted by cupellation from lead ore which was widespread in Britain, although the silver content was low. The richness of the deposits was emphasized by Pliny, who wrote that lead occurs 'in Britain on the surface so freely that there is actually a law against its being exploited beyond a certain amount'. It was found especially in the Mendip Hills of Somerset, in Salop, Clwyd (Flint), Derbyshire and the West Riding of Yorkshire. The Romans, as we have seen (p. 55), lost no time in exploiting these riches, the earliest ingot being dated AD 49. At first the army undertook the work, but thereafter, except in military areas, mining rights were leased by a *procurator metallorum* to *conductores*, who were either imperial freedmen or businessmen operating alone or in companies (*societates*). One such imperial freedman, mentioned above (p. 57), was Triferna at Lutudarum in Derbyshire. But under Hadrian the Derby ingots were stamped with the name of the mine as well as the emperor's name (METALLUM LUTUDARENSE), which suggests the imposition of greater imperial regulation, while the army continued to exercise control in military areas, for instance at the Antonine fort at Brough in Derbyshire, and again in the third century at Alston in Northumberland. Since the latest inscribed ingots from the Mendips belong to AD 164–9, imperial working may have slackened off, but private interests continued, and these may be reflected in the good quality of the late fourth-century silver coins from this district. At the Mendip mines a settlement developed at Charterhouse, which even had a small amphitheatre to keep the miners entertained.

If Caesar, when he said that the Britons used imported *aes*, was referring to copper, he was probably right: evidence is lacking for Iron Age pre-Roman workings, and copper may have been imported even in the Bronze Age, to be worked into bronze with British tin. The Romans, however, began to exploit the copper mines in Anglesey, North Wales and Shropshire. The metal was worked into bun-shaped ingots of some 30–50 lb, of which eighteen have been found in Anglesey and Caernarvonshire. Those that are stamped give the names of individuals or companies rather than the emperor's, which indicates that the mines must have been worked by private lessees. At the mines on the Great Orme's Head, inhabited caves have been found with objects from the third and fourth centuries, while at Llanymynech in Shropshire coins of Antoninus Pius and Constantine occur, together with skeletons. These cave-dwellers could have been slave or convict labourers who worked the mines, unless they were refugees in late Roman times. In Anglesey, the ore seems to have been smelted near by, but local smelting has not been traced on the Great Orme. The desire to protect

A blacksmith working at his forge appears on a tombstone relief from York.

the mines may have been one factor in the Roman decision to continue to hold on to their forts at Holyhead and at Caernarvon (Segontium) until AD 383. Copper was hardly ever used in its pure state, but made into bronze or brass by alloying with tin, zinc, or lead. The manufacture of bronze objects became an important element in the economy of the island.

Iron mines were worked on a considerable scale, and iron was being exported to the Continent by Strabo's day. The main areas were the Weald in Sussex (this explains Caesar's remark that iron was found in coastal areas), the Forest of Dean, parts of the Midlands, and North Wales. In the Weald some large furnace-sites have been discovered, consisting of cinder-heaps 50 feet high and two acres in extent; this slag provided the Romans with material for local road-making. At Weston-under-Penyard (Ariconium) in the Forest of Dean, slag-heaps covered 200 acres, and coins indicate activity from the late first century until the fourth. At Lydney, Glos., the miners appear to have lived from the second till the late fourth century in huts on the top of a hill which was riddled with galleries. Iron-mining was not an imperial monopoly, though the government could, of course, direct labour where it wished. Thus in the north there are several examples to show that iron was produced locally for the use of the garrisons in forts. At Corbridge, for example, iron was brought in from Risingham (Habitancum) and worked by the legionaries in a military arsenal. In addition, roof-tiles stamped CLASSIS BRITANNICA and found in connection with slag in the Weald suggest official interest by the Roman navy and possibly naval workshops. Technically, Roman production with shaft-furnaces was a great advance on the primitive bowl-furnaces of pre-Roman days, and there is no doubt that the iron industry was of great importance, supplying many of the tools and implements of daily life.

Coal too was mined, mainly from surface outcrops, especially in Somerset and the southwest, and in military areas in the north. It is mentioned once only in literature, when Solinus, a third-century writer, noted as a curiosity that coal was to be seen on the altars of Sul Minerva at Bath (Aquae Sulis). At Housesteads, about a ton was found in a guard chamber, and even more in the bath building at Risingham. In fact it was regularly exploited and carted to Roman forts on both the Hadrianic and Antonine Walls from the mid-second century until the fourth. Its main use was for heating baths and hypocausts in forts and villas. Wood or charcoal were generally used as fuels; coal contained more sulphur than was desirable for iron-smelting, but it was used if necessary, and also for smelting lead and glass.

Other minerals served more artistic purposes. Kimmeridge shale from Dorset was worked into jewellery, decorative panels and furniture (e.g. table legs). The hard marble of Purbeck (Dorset) was used for grinding-mortars, and also for tablets for important inscriptions throughout southern and central Britain. Jet from Whitby, Yorks., was popular for ornamental jewellery such as hairpins, rings, bracelets and necklaces, and gained an almost magical reputation for its magnetic properties. Other jewels were adorned with pearls, the British variety being well thought of, though considered a trifle too dusky.

The quarrying of stone for building must have increased sharply both during the first century, as the process of town-building accelerated, and also later when stone replaced half-timbered houses, town walls were built, and villas proliferated. Good stone was available in most parts of Britain: the walls of London were built of Kentish rag from Maidstone; flint was used in the southeast; limestones from the Cotswolds, Northamptonshire and Lincolnshire were popular; red sandstone was used at Chester and sent to Caernarvon for the rebuilding of the fort there, though later local stone was used. The luxury-loving rich could import finer marble and alabaster.

Two other natural products of great importance were timber and salt. Timber was widely needed by the army and also for house-building, while salt, which in early days was obtained by boiling sea-water, was of course essential. Salt-works (clay floors heated by flues) are found around the southern and eastern coasts, and the salt springs at Droitwich gave its name of Salinae to the town.

THE PRODUCTS OF INDUSTRY

So far the nature and distribution of raw materials have been emphasized, rather than their uses as objects of manufacture. To this we must now turn. In pre-Roman days the beautiful ornaments and weapons made for the Celtic aristocracy can be contrasted with the simpler objects made by the peasants themselves for everyday use. Even before the Roman conquest, native luxury work was being supplemented by imported articles which gradually thereafter tended to swamp production in the native tradition. A certain number of foreign workers came over to the island to practise their crafts, while some native workers began to imitate the new models. Roman influences were also felt in the cruder products for the local peasant markets, and native workmen were now heirs to two traditions.

The products of the metal industries are fairly obvious and do not need much description. Some at least of the gold objects found in Britain were made locally: for instance an inscription from Malton, Yorks., reads: 'Good luck to the Genius of this place; young slave, use to your good fortune this goldsmith's shop.' In some metal-workers' shops at St Albans small crucibles containing gold have been found. Silver was used for spoons, and also for plating bronze objects. Some inscribed silver plates used as votive offerings have been found, but much of the best silverwork found in Britain was imported. This includes two magnificent hoards: the marvellous silver dish (nearly two feet in diameter) and other objects found at Mildenhall, Suffolk, in the 1940s, and the Christian silverware buried c. AD 350 and discovered at Water Newton, Huntingdonshire, in 1975. These can only have belonged to exceedingly rich families. The former, it has been conjectured, might have been a gift to Lupicinus, a general sent to Britain by the emperor Julian in AD 360 to stem a barbarian attack. Its place of manufacture is equally uncertain, though Constantinople is a possibility.

Much of the silver produced in Britain must have been retained officially for use in the mints. Lead on the other hand was widely used for water-pipes, cisterns, coffins and burial urns: for example an inscribed pipe records the installation of a water supply for the legionary fortress at Chester by Agricola

A Romano-British glass
flagon from Bayford, Kent.

in AD 79: 'In the ninth consulship of the emperor Vespasian and the seventh
of Titus, under Gnaeus Julius Agricola, governor [*legatus Augusti pro
praetore*].'

In the bronze industry we can trace the Celtic and Roman traditions more
clearly. Local or itinerant craftsmen in the north and west still produced
work in the Celtic tradition, which included dragonesque or trumpet-type
brooches and bronze cauldrons. For the towns, however, bronze objects in
the classical tradition were made by immigrant artists and then by natives
who copied these models, though works of the finest craftsmanship were still
imported. At first a considerable variety of brooches was manufactured, with
many local characteristics, but from the late second century onwards they

became more uniform. Sporadic evidence survives for the smelting of the raw materials – copper and tin – in crucibles, and the casting of this into clay or stone moulds: thus a bronze-smithy has been found at Heronbridge near Chester.

Glass-works have been located at Wilderspool in Lancashire, Caistor-by-Norwich, and Mancetter in Warwickshire: remains include furnaces, crucibles, glass scum and waste, and pieces of finished glass. These sites produced window glass, but finer glass ware was imported from Syria and Alexandria in the first century, and later from the Rhineland and France.

Pottery survives in vast quantities. While the best pottery, commonly called Samian ware, was imported, everyday coarse ware was manufactured throughout the whole country to supply local needs. Where clays were especially good, local potteries might extend the range of their business and certain wares were distributed more widely. Two of the most important of these were Castor ware and New Forest ware. The former was made in the area of the Nene valley in Northamptonshire from the late second century, and a potter's workshop has recently been found at Stibbington. Castor ware decoration was applied manually by the barbotine method, and depicted lively hunting scenes with animals or foliate scrolls. It was appreciated to the extent of being distributed to all parts of Britain, and also exported to the Rhineland. The New Forest potteries, which were active in the late third and fourth centuries, characteristically displayed a dark metallic surface, often with painted ornament. The organization of the two centres differed: at Castor the industry rested on a capitalist basis with manufacturers living in

A shallow Samian ware bowl found at London. This red-coated ware, imported in great quantities throughout the Roman period, mainly from Gaul, was more sophisticated and elegant than the native product.

Examples of local pottery:
above, a Castor ware
(Cambridgeshire) beaker
with a chariot race in
barbotine, from Colchester.
Right, New Forest ware, an
indented beaker.

large houses, surrounded by the smaller dwellings of their workmen and by elaborate kilns. In the New Forest the potters appear to have been independent workers who lived in temporary quarters, using small primitive kilns and moving on to other sites when their local fuel supply gave out. Nevertheless their wares managed to find markets all over the south of England.

In earlier days before these more specialized wares were produced, the need for good quality pottery was met by import. Even before the Roman conquest, red-glazed pottery from Arezzo in Italy was beginning to adorn the tables of some richer Britons, but in the first century AD a flood of Samian pottery from Gallic factories dominated the markets. A ship with a full cargo of this ware was wrecked off the coast of Kent at Pudding Pan Rock in the late second century while on its way to London. Attempts at imitation were made by some native British potters, but these were not very successful. Some Rhenish ware, too, was imported from the district of Cologne. But when the Gallic industry was badly damaged in 197 in the struggle between Severus and Albinus, the rebel governor of Britain, the importation of Samian ware sharply declined. Now the way was open for the growth of good native production such as Castor ware, which continued down to the early fifth century, or a red-colour coated ware from Oxfordshire potteries. All this time, of course, local potters throughout the country were pouring out their everyday ware.

Potters who secured army contracts were especially lucky. In the early days of the occupation the army units had their own kilns, but soon they began to use native manufacture: for example, a large proportion of the bowls (*mortaria*) from the Antonine Wall came from kilns at Colchester or the Midlands. But though much of the work must have been in the hands of natives, the stimulus came from foreign capital. We hear of seven Roman citizens (probably freedmen) who produced stamped *mortaria* at Colchester in Flavian-Trajanic days, while a certain C. Attius Marinus worked at Colchester, moved on to Radlett near St Albans, and finally settled to work at Hartshill in Warwickshire.

The need for bricks and tiles developed on a large scale only with the Roman occupation, so this industry tended to be more Roman in character. The army, both legions and auxiliaries, had their own tile-works, with the products stamped with the name of the unit, such as the II, VI, IX and XX legions, or the *classis Britannica*. The factory of Legio XX at Holt in Denbighshire covers some 20 acres, and includes workshops, barracks and a bath-house for the workers supplied by the legion. This contrasts with the small tilery at Pen-y-Stryd near the fort at Tomen-y-Mur. At Silchester there was an imperial tilery run by procurators, as shown by a stamp of Nero:'Ner(onis) Cl(audii) Cae(saris) Aug(usti) Ger(manici).' Some towns also had their own municipal works, as at Gloucester: 'r(es) p(ublica) G(levensium)', and the tile-stamps of many private makers have been found in different parts of the country.

Spinning and weaving long remained a domestic occupation for the women of a household, and spindle-whorls and loom-weights have been widely found. Gradually, however, textile industries developed, and Diocletian's Price Edict refers to British cloth as a commercial export to the Eastern empire. There is also a reference in an official list (the *Notitia Dignitatum*) to 'the imperial manager of the weaving-works in Britain at Venta'. Although the existence of what once appeared to be large-scale fulling establishments in some villas, such as Chedworth, has now been questioned, tanks in a villa at Darenth in Kent may well be connected with fulling or dyeing, and some textile production perhaps exceeded merely local needs even before state factories were set up in the fourth century.

Not much is known about the production of leather, which was needed in quantity by both soldiers and civilians for clothing, shoes, tents, harness and the like. But a quantity of cattle bones points to a tanning industry at Silchester, and another deposit of bones outside the fort at Catterick shows that the army was looking after its own leather supply in the period AD 80–120.

TRADE

It is clear that Britain enjoyed a fairly lively internal trade in some manufactured goods, especially in metals and pottery, but the island had to face problems in her external commerce. In the pre-Roman period the demand by British chiefs for foreign luxury goods must have stimulated the production of native materials which would pay for the imports. As we have seen (p. 32), Strabo lists Britain's surplus products in Augustus' day, but during the second half of the first century AD the demand for luxury objects increased with the spread of Roman habits. True, the products of agriculture and the metal industries may have expanded, but the army absorbed the increasing supply of corn, while the exploitation of the mineral wealth primarily enriched the Roman government, since metals belonged to the state. Thus, at first, financial pressures led to much borrowing and debt, such as helped to promote Boudicca's revolt. Nero's minister, Seneca, alone had 10,000,000 sesterces on loan in Britain. But gradually British workmen began to produce more goods acceptable in the home market, so that by the Antonine period Britain had come much nearer to self-sufficiency.

In the third century British pottery largely replaced foreign imports, the pewter industry increased (though a few very plutocratic families still imported silverware), the state may have allowed local enterprise a greater share in the exploitation of the lead mines, the production of wine and beer probably increased in southern Britain, and life in the villas gradually became more self-sufficient. As a result, the island's economy became more balanced as less wealth was drained away, and was helped by the steady export of those surplus objects mentioned by Strabo, to which may be added a few specialized luxury objects, such as ornaments of Whitby jet. In a panegyric addressed to Constantius at the end of the third century the speaker refers to Britain as 'a land with such a wealth of fruits, rejoicing in such a number of pastures, abounding in veins of ores, so profitable in its revenues, surrounded by so many harbours, so vast in its circuit', and a little later another writer, referring to the visit of St Germanus, describes Britain as 'a most wealthy island' (*opulentissima insula*). Some exaggeration there may be, but Britain had clearly become prosperous in the later days of Roman occupation, and was soon to be a magnet to the Saxons.

Trade was not confined to the Roman world, but spread over the frontier to Scotland and even, to a very limited extent, across the sea to Ireland. Trade to Scotland was controlled by a post on Hadrian's Wall, while other goods were carried up the east and west coasts (until Irish raiders in the fourth century made the western route too hazardous). Goods imported into Scotland included pottery and glass, some of which had already been previously imported into Britain, as well as bronze and iron objects and some wine. In return, Britain received valuable slaves, cattle, hides, furs, wild animals, and perhaps wool. Trade with Ireland was on a much smaller scale and was paid for in cash rather than by means of exports. Roman coins are found on the east coast, and they may well have been used to purchase slaves and cattle.

Trade depends on communications and transport, and here we come to one of Rome's greatest and most enduring gifts to Britain – her road system. Designed in the first place for military needs, the roads served commercial interests and united the country in a network of communications. These great metalled highways, some 20–24 feet wide and marked out by milestones, were well drained and maintained throughout the year. They

Opposite above, a stretch of original Roman roadway at Wheeldale Moor, Yorks., showing the foundation layer and a drainage channel. *Below*, the many-layered surface was built to last, as shown in this cross-section.

cobbles of 3rd period road

clay

clay   clay

remetalling or 2nd period road

cobbles and gravel

sand

quarry stones

hard gravel

quarry stones

yellow sand or chippings

clay

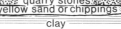

0   20 ft

Roman transport: a team of
mules draws a cart and
passengers past a milestone.

were complemented by widespread local road systems, which included the
old ridgeways. The chief method of transport was a four-wheeled cart, such as
is often depicted on sculptures in Gaul. Road transport was supplemented by
water-borne traffic on rivers, canals such as Car Dyke in East Anglia, and
coastal shipping. Dover, with its lighthouses, became the main base for cross-
Channel shipping, and voyages might be made direct to the mouths of the
Seine, Loire, Garonne and Rhine. London soon established itself as the chief
port in the southeast, as well as the centre of the road system.

Trade also required coinage. This antedated the Roman conquest: the
Britons copied the coins of northern Gaul which, as we have seen, displayed
Celtic abstract adaptations of the naturalistic Greek coinage of Philip II of
Macedon. Under Roman influences, however, the pendulum began to swing
back again, and Cunobelinus went so far as to name himself 'king' in Latin
(REX) on some of his coins. Soon the official Roman coinage, imported from
the mints in Rome and Lyons, began to circulate in the island. At first a
shortage led to some native copies, but in the second century it was universal,
and all native coinage had died out. This imperial coinage consisted of gold
(*aurei*), silver (*denarii*) and brass (*sestertii* and *asses*). During the inflation which
struck the whole Roman world in the third century, when debased coins

proliferated, local coins of varied standards appeared once again. In the empire as a whole, various emperors made valiant efforts to restore confidence in the currency, and this was achieved when Constantine introduced a new gold coin, the *solidus* (*c.* AD 312).

During the chaotic days of the third century, mints had sprung up in various places. Carausius established an official mint in London, with a second probably at Bitterne (Clausentum), near Southampton. The London mint continued to issue intermittently, and its copper went on till about 325. However, much of the coinage for the western provinces was now minted at Trier. Trade and commerce received great stimulus from the introduction of a uniform and generally stable currency; periods of financial uncertainty merely reflected the ills of the Roman empire as a whole.

Coins, though designed primarily for economic purposes, were also a means of spreading, especially among the illiterate, some of the aspects of the benefits and achievements of imperial rule which the emperors wished to circulate through the provinces. Thus various events in the history of Britain were commemorated on the coinage: the conquest by Claudius (an equestrian statue of the emperor on a triumphal arch: DE BRITANNIS); the building of both the Walls (Britannia on guard, seated on the Wall); Hadrian's visit (Britannia greeting the emperor); Caracalla's successful northern campaign (a trophy: VICTORIAE BRITANNICAE); and on the famous Arras medal, the personification of London welcoming Constantius with gratitude for his timely rescue (see p. 69). In addition there are more general subjects, proclaiming the virtues of emperors and the blessings of peace.

'Restorer of Eternal Light': the Arras medal, a commemorative medallion of *c.* AD 296, depicts the emperor Constantius as the saviour of Britain following Carausius' usurpation.

The traders who kept the economy going are tantalizingly glimpsed in a few inscriptions. We know the names of three merchants who appear to have been engaged in the wine trade: M. Aurelius Lunaris, a priest of the imperial cult (*sevir Augustalis*) at both York and Lincoln (see p. 90), dedicated an altar at Bordeaux in gratitude for a safe journey from York in AD 237; M. Verecundius Diogenes, another *sevir* from York, where his tombstone was found, came from Bourges and may well have been an importer of wine; L. Solimarius Secundus, who came from Trier and was buried at Bordeaux, was described as a British merchant (*negotiator Britannicianus*). A third York *sevir*, also describing himself as *negotiator Britannicianus*, was Lucius Viducius Placidus, a pottery merchant (*cretarius*?) from Rouen, who dedicated an altar, found in the East Scheldt estuary, to a goddess named Nehalennia. An inscription found at York in 1976 records a further dedication by him, dated to AD 221, to 'Jupiter Dolichenus . . . to the Genius of the Place and to the emperors'.

Two Oriental merchants are represented: a certain Salmanes, who died at Auchendavy on the Antonine Wall, and whose Semitic name suggests he was a Syrian trader; and Barates from Palmyra, who set up an elaborate tomb to his wife at South Shields. She is depicted seated and holding her work-basket, distaff and jewel box, and the inscription tells us that she had been a

Relics of the wine trade: Roman barrels found lining a well at Silchester.

142

Regina, British wife of a Levantine (Palmyrean) businessman. Her tombstone was found at South Shields, near the Wall.

Catuvellaunian whom Barates had freed and named Regina. The richness of the tombstone suggests that he must have been a prosperous merchant. We know of a certain Barates, buried at Corbridge, who is described as *vexillarius*. If this means 'flag-bearer' he will have been a soldier and not our merchant, but it is just possible that the meaning is 'flag-maker', in which case he might be the same man.

From London come three glimpses of commercial life in the city. Scratched on a jug are the words, 'London; next door to the temple of Isis', thus indicating the address of the jug's owner, probably an inn-keeper at Southwark. On surviving wooden writing-tablets which were originally covered with wax three rather incoherent notes can be read: 'This money when the applications have been written again will be owed to me by Crescens or the party concerned; payment due: [on the Ides?].'

'To have sold goods . . . from his own shop . . . a ship to be built and to have permission given . . . of making a rudder.' '[Dated] from London. Luita to his [partners?]. Rufus son of Callisunus sends greeting to Epillicus and all his partners. I believe you know that I am well. If you have gone to law, please send me all the details. See to it that you turn that girl into cash.'

This last reference is a reminder that in both town and country much depended on the labour of slaves, though the extent of slavery cannot be estimated. We know the names of some of the more favoured slaves, but little about the conditions of the majority, which must have varied greatly: treatment in the mines would have been brutally harsh, whereas work on the farm or in the household would have depended considerably on the temper of the owner. But as in the course of time the supply of slaves began to dwindle, so their treatment may have improved, if only because their commercial value was becoming greater.

Finally, we may note some graffiti, scribbled on wet clay by workers, free or slave, before the pot or tile was fired. Written in Latin, they provide striking testimony to the process of Romanization. One man complains about a fellow worker: 'Austalis has been wandering about by himself every day for a fortnight'. Some refer to work completed: 'Clementinus made this box-tile'; 'Primus has made ten'. When the word 'satis' occurs it may indicate either a job well done or that the maker has done enough and is fed up. At Dover one workman scrawled, 'I made 550 box-tiles', to which another had added the words, 'I smashed 51'. One man just jotted down his name and the date: 'Sixth day before the Kalends of October. Manuiccus.' Another wrote of his girl ' . . . puellam . . .'. Lastly we should mention a more literary effort, a quotation from the beginning of the second book of Virgil's *Aeneid* emerging from a jumble of phrases: '*Conticuere omnes*' (They all fell silent).

We have abundant evidence for such professional activities as education and medicine in the Roman world in general, but unfortunately very little direct evidence from Roman Britain. An inscription, written in Greek, records that a doctor named Hermogenes set up an altar at Chester to 'the mighty Saviour Gods'; many physicians at this time were Greeks. We also have several dedications to Aesculapius, the god of healing. Thus a tribune dedicated an altar to the god at Lanchester with an inscription in both Greek and Latin, *c.* AD 175, and at Chester the freedmen and house slaves (*liberti et familia*) of a high Roman official (the governor or a legionary legate) made their offering to 'Fortune the Home-bringer, to Aesculapius and to Salus'. Other such dedications come from South Shields, Maryport and Overborough, Lancs. Other inscriptions refer to army doctors.

A considerable number of surgical instruments survive: at London and Silchester we find scalpels, probes, artery forceps, and tongue depressors. One aspect of medicine, eye trouble, is illustrated by a disproportionate amount of surviving evidence, since we have well over 20 prescriptions by opticians; these take the form of inscribed small stone slabs. Thus Gaius Valerius Amandus offered 'a vinegar lotion for running eyes [*ad rheumatica*]', 'drops for dim sight [*ad caliginem*]', 'poppy ointment for an attack of inflammation [*lippitudo*]', as well as a mixture for clearing the sight (*ad claritudinem*). Other stamps found in 1973 in Chester prescribe drops (*stactum*), anti-irritant (*diapsoricum*), ointments (*penicilli*) and saffron salve for soreness (*crocades ad aspritudinem*). Since similar stamps have a wide distribution, opticians were apparently to be found in various parts of the country, and eye troubles were prevalent. One British oculist, named Stolus, became famous enough for his eye salve (*collyrium*) to be mentioned by Galen, the last great physician of antiquity. Finally, a graffito on a cinerary urn from Buckinghamshire appears to record (in Greek) a *mulophysicus*: if this is the correct reading, we have evidence for a 'mule-doctor', a veterinary physician, who may well have tended transport animals.

9

Language, art and religion

LATIN AND CELTIC

The spread of Roman culture in Britain, and its intermingling with the native tradition, can be traced to some extent in the areas of language, art and religion. At one end of the social range was the peasant, illiterate and speaking only Celtic, while at the other was the civilized administrator, who would have been well versed in Latin and Greek literature, speaking both languages fluently. How quickly and how far down the social scale such culture extended can only be surmised, but we can assume that many of the town-dwellers of southeast Britain must have had a smattering of Latin before the Claudian invasion, thanks to commercial contacts, and during the period of conquest it became official Roman policy to promote Romanization. Agricola, as we have seen (p. 47), appreciated the Briton's natural ability, encouraging the use of Latin and training the sons of the chiefs in the liberal arts. Schools must have been set up, with the traditional Roman education in language, literature and rhetoric. One Greek schoolmaster, whom Agricola appears to have brought from Tarsus to Britain, was a certain Demetrius. Plutarch, who later met him at Delphi, learnt from Demetrius that he had served on a mission to the remoter British isles (on Agricola's reconnaissance in 82?), when incidentally he had come across a community of 'holy men' who lived unmolested by the warlike peoples around them, and who told Demetrius their ideas about meteorology and mythology. This Demetrius is probably the man who made dedications at York (in Greek) 'to the gods of the governor's *praetorium*' as well as to Ocean and Tethys. At about the same time, the satirist Juvenal was writing: 'Eloquent Gaul has taught the Britons to plead a case; by now distant Thule talks of hiring a rhetorician.' And the poet Martial acclaimed a British lady, Claudia Rufina, who 'though sprung from the woad-stained Britons has the spirit of the Latin race' (by Flavian times the woad-stained Briton was probably something of a literary cliché).

Beside being officially encouraged, the use of Latin must have been extended through growing contact with all ranks of the Roman army (who were becoming an increasingly cosmopolitan group), as well as with the colonies of Roman citizens and visiting merchants and traders. Such people of course all spoke Latin in its everyday form ('Vulgar' Latin), and not the formal language of the classical writers. It has been suggested that the Latin spoken in Britain was slightly purer than the Vulgar Latin of the other western provinces, perhaps because much of it was first learnt in the schools.

The use of Latin by the army has recently been illustrated by the important wooden writing-tablets found in or near the *praetorium* of the fort at

Opposite, a Romano-British deity discovered at Southwark Cathedral, 1977, possibly Apollo-Maponus.

Vindolanda (see p. 84); fragments of letters and legal documents have also been preserved on other such tablets, as we have seen. More significant evidence, however, for the spread of Latin are the graffiti scratched by workmen on tiles. These include a date given in the ordinary Roman way 'VI. k. octo.' (26 September), and a quotation from the *Aeneid* which, together with some other words, may be part of a writing lesson. A tile from Caerwent, which shows the name Bellicanus written in four different hands, may also represent a writing lesson. Thus many people in the towns learnt to speak Latin. Peasants and small farmers would no doubt have kept entirely to Celtic, but the well-to-do landowners would have turned to Latin. No written traces of British survive, probably because a majority of the rural population remained illiterate. British Celtic was the language of the countryside; in the towns many probably spoke both British and Latin; and the governing class added Greek to their native Latin.

But however widely Latin was used for some 400 years, its roots did not sink so deep as in France and Spain. It did not survive to become a Romance language, but succumbed to the incoming flood of Anglo-Saxons, although by other channels (not least the Church) it was later to return to help form modern English. However, in the highland zone, especially in Wales, Cornwall and Cumbria, British Celtic survived. By this time the Celts had in fact absorbed quite a number of Latin words, both where their own vocabulary seemed deficient in coping with new ideas and concepts, and also for some more ordinary aspects of daily life. These words, at least 600 in number, vividly reveal the impact of Rome on the natives of Britain and cover such topics as agriculture, the sea and shipping, building, cooking and eating, washing, education, intellectual life, public affairs, military and religious matters.

	Latin	Welsh	English
AGRICULTURE	furca	fforch	pitchfork
	frenum	ffrwyna	bridle
	praesepe	preseb	manger
	mola	melin	mill
	puteus	pydew	well
	grex	gyr	herd
	oleum	olew	oil
	vinea	givinwydden	vine

and words for cherry, chestnut, rose, violet, poppy and lily.

	Latin	Welsh	English
SEA AND SHIPPING	mare	mor	sea
	ancora	angor	anchor
	portus	porth	harbour
BUILDING	murus	mur	wall
	fenestra	ffenester	window
	pons	pont	bridge
	vitrum	gwydr	glass

COOKING	cucina	cegin	kitchen
	cultellus	cyllell	knife
	furnus	ffwrn	oven
	taberna	tafarn	inn
WASHING	sapo	seban	soap
	sponga	ysbwng	sponge
EDUCATION AND	auctor	awdur	author
INTELLECTUAL LIFE	orator	arawd	orator
	medicus	meddyg	doctor
	schola	ysgol	school
	scribere	ysgrifennu	to write
PUBLIC LIFE	civitas	ciwdod	tribe
	populus	pobl	people
	testis	tyst	witness
	fides	ffydd	faith
MILITARY	arma	arf	weapons
	castellum	castell	castle
	miles	milwyr	soldier
	imperator	ymerawdwr	commander

There are numerous religious words, especially from Christian Latin.

A mere glance at these words must impress the reader with the impact of Latin on British-Celtic, and the survival of so much in the Welsh language, which began to develop on its own lines in the latest stages of the Roman occupation: a language in which bards were soon to celebrate the exploits of their heroes. In this they were presumably carrying on older practices, since the Celts were always known for their love of music and oral literary composition. If the Celts ever gathered to enjoy a British Eisteddfod, they have unfortunately left no trace of it.

Some Latin apparently continued to be spoken in the second half of the fifth century as far west as Wroxeter, where the epitaph of an Irishman of about that date was found in 1967. It reads, 'Cunorix Macus [son of] MaquiColine.' Whether Cunorix was an Irish invader or a settler, it is interesting that Latin letters and not the Ogam script were chosen for the inscription, though the Celtic word for son, *macus*, was used instead of *filius*. Furthermore, since the stone was found in a cemetery area just outside the eastern defences of Wroxeter, this may imply that the town had not contracted much by this late date, if burial outside towns was still the custom. So the stone casts light on both linguistic and possibly urban survival.

Only towards the last days of Roman Britain do we hear of any British writers. Ausonius of Bordeaux refers slightingly to a British poet, Silvius Bonus, to the effect that no Briton could be good (*bonus*) despite his name. The talents of two British Christian writers were very different. St Patrick complained that he could not write good Latin, because he had not spoken it in childhood and had been kidnapped by Irish raiders at the age of 16 (c. AD 405). On the other hand, Pelagius had received an excellent education in both classical and Christian literature before he left Britain soon after AD 380 to study law at Rome. Moreover, the educated owners of villas liked to be reminded of their Virgil: references to the poet survive in some mosaics and wall-paintings. By the time of the British monk Gildas, who in the sixth century could refer to Latin as 'our language' (*nostra lingua*), and the 'Venerable' Bede, we are moving into another age.

ART

The cultural, social and religious life of Roman Britain obviously found its expression in the art which flourished there for a period of 400 years. But this was a great mixture, with some objects produced locally and others imported from abroad. Two very different streams of artistic tradition were thereby represented – the native Celtic and the imperial Roman – and the significance attached to each has been very variously assessed. An extreme view is that of R. G. Collingwood, who argued that a flourishing native Celtic art was strangled by a rather second-rate foreign artistic tradition. Then, after lying dormant for four centuries, it re-emerged when the heavy hand of Rome had been removed. A more balanced view is that there was some genuine interplay between the two traditions, and that in the process there emerged some artistic production which, although predominantly 'Roman', nevertheless represented a blend with native art, and so can legitimately be called Romano-British.

Of the two elements the Celtic is the simpler to define. We have already seen how an imaginative non-representational art was flourishing in the late Iron Age, and was being subjected to increasing Roman influences during the century between Julius Caesar and Claudius. Some would argue that aesthetically it was already passing its peak, and that a decline was natural when the tribal warrior aristocracy for which it catered began to alter. However, it lingered on in the highland zone. Roman art on the other hand is more complex: the phrase can be applied either to works produced in Rome and Italy which reflected her national tradition, or more widely to the diversified forms which developed in the various provinces of the empire.

Right from its commencement, however, all this artistic production was permeated by Greek artistic ideas; even in the sixth century BC the emergent city of Rome came under strong Greek artistic influences, whether from contact with the Greek cities of southern Italy or through the Etruscans, whose own art owed so much to the Greeks. Indeed, not only was Roman imperial art based on Greek ideas, although often infused with a sturdy Roman independence of thought, but a great deal of it was actually produced by Greek artists. As it spread more widely through the provinces, it was naturally affected in varying degree by native traditions, and we should remember that its contact with Celtic art was first made in Gaul, and only later in Britain. But Gaulish artists and works of art often crossed the Channel, and these works were frequently imitated by native craftsmen, so it is not always easy to distinguish the precise origin of some of the objects found in Britain. However, through the work of immigrant and native British artists a certain amalgam was achieved between the abstract Celtic and naturalistic Graeco-Roman traditions.

Thus objects found in Roman Britain have a very varied background. Sculptures carved in Mediterranean marbles by artists from Mediterranean lands were imported, such as the statues found in the London Mithraeum, and the marble busts at Lullingstone. Even if such works were ordered by non-British inhabitants, their presence in Britain afforded examples for native craftsmen to copy, and so stimulated the growth of a Romano-British tradition in a field not entered by Celtic artists. In fact the introduction into Britain of the human figure as a principal subject for art is one of the major developments in the island's artistic history. From Gaul came many bronze statues and statuettes, some silver work, and Samian ware, together with most of the terracotta figurines and glass vessels found here. Foreign workers, whether visitors or settlers, were responsible for laying most of the best mosaics (though made of British stones) and some of the paintings. The sculpture needed by the Roman army for votive and funerary purposes was probably produced by artists attached to the forces or settled as colonists. Some of these works, such as the tombstone of Facilis at Colchester mentioned earlier, are excellent, others are much cruder, and as time went on local carvers may have been used. During the second and third centuries many excellent sculptures in British stone were produced locally by immigrant Gaulish artists, so that a Celtic-Roman style emerged.

Finally there are the British-born artists. These are difficult to identify, since even in the rare cases when their works are signed, for example the fine figured bronze skillet-handle from the Isle of Ely, signed by Bodvogenus, we cannot be sure whether the artist was a Briton or a Gaul. But many small metal objects which are in line with the late La Tène Celtic tradition may be assigned to British workmen, and so may most of the objects carved in Kimmeridge shale or Yorkshire jet. Some mosaic pavements were laid by natives who used the copy-books which circulated widely in the empire: these supplied the main composition, but left the local artist freedom to extemporize in detail. Various schools of mosaicists have been distinguished, perhaps as many as ten. Then, of course, there was the very great quantity of locally produced pottery, including the excellent Castor ware from near Peterborough, which sometimes outdoes its continental models.

Thus the art of Roman Britain showed great variety, although based essentially on classical traditions. Its wide range cannot be illustrated here, still less that of architecture, though some aspects have been mentioned in other contexts elsewhere in this book. However, a few items of the more distinctively native Romano-British art claim attention. Most famous is the relief for the temple of the Celtic goddess, Sulis-Minerva, at Bath, which combines her Medusa-like head with that of the water god of the Avon near by. The design is classical: a large circular shield contains within two concentric oak wreaths the wild 'Gorgon' head of the goddess. It is held on either side by a flying Victory whose feet rest on a globe, and each is flanked by a Triton. But the flowing draperies of the Victories and the wild glaring face of the goddess with her snaky locks are not in the Roman tradition. The

British masterpieces resulting from the fusion of Celtic and classical: *right*, the famous Medusa head, moustached, from the temple of Minerva at Bath; *below*, a fourth-century head of Constantine from York, where he was first proclaimed emperor; *below right*, head of Antenociticus, a native god honoured at a small temple in Benwell, on the Wall.

Roman British art from Hadrian's Wall: stone carving of a lion from Corbridge (Corstopitum); *below*, statue of Juno Regina from Chesters, Northumberland.

artist was a Celt, be he Gaul or Briton, and he has injected a true Celtic spirit into a Roman setting. Indeed he may well have been either of two artists known at Bath: 'Priscus, son of Toutus, a stone-mason [*lapidarius*], citizen of the Carnutes' (i.e. near Chartres) or the Briton 'Sulinus, son of Bracetus, the sculptor' (misspelt *scultor*!).

From Benwell on Hadrian's Wall comes a remarkable stone head of the god Antenociticus which is clearly Celtic in inspiration: a certain wildness of the hair and a somewhat other-worldly look is combined with a more classical style. A similar fusion of classical and Celtic traits is shown in a male head from Gloucester, and a girl's head from Otterbourne, Hants. In both, realism and impressionism go hand in hand. Again, a stately statue of Juno Regina from Chesters shows a Roman figure, but one whose draperies reveal the hand of a Celt, whether British or Gaulish. The well-known Corbridge lion, standing over a helpless stag, is an intensely vital piece of work, solidly three-dimensional but with face, paws and tail treated in non-representational manner. The vigour of the lion contrasts strongly with the limp form of his flattened victim. Two other lions, made of bronze, from Capel St Mary in Suffolk, are partly representational, but their tails and stylized manes are Celtic. Beside sculptors, many potters show a real Celtic element in their work. In Castor ware (unlike the mass-produced Samian pottery) the decoration was applied separately by each potter, by the so-called barbotine method which afforded scope for the individual's ability and predilections. These artists were not so successful when they portrayed the human figure, whether huntsmen or gladiators, but they excelled in flowing scenes of spirited elongated dogs chasing hares amid spirals, scrolls and tendrils in the true Celtic spirit.

Thus Celtic art remained strong enough to infuse a genuine native spirit into many classical forms of art, and continued in a purer form in unconquered Scotland and Ireland. How far it influenced early Anglo-Saxon art is a much debated question, but during the 400 years of Roman occupation the art found throughout the greater part of Britain, in town and country, in mansion, villa or even cottage, was predominantly Roman and classical in style.

ROMAN DEITIES AND THE IMPERIAL CULT

The religious beliefs and practices of the Celts in early Britain have already been sketched out. These probably continued with little change in the remoter country districts throughout the Roman period, but elsewhere they were fused, to a considerable extent, with the cults which the Romans brought with them. In order to understand this fusion we should first glance at the basic religious ideas of the Romans. In very early times, say about 1000 BC, these may not have been altogether different from those of the Celts, but by the time of the Roman occupation of Britain they had progressed and changed a great deal. Since the Romans were polytheistic, they were ready to accept any new gods that they might encounter during their expansion in the Mediterranean world, so when they came into contact with Celts no serious religious clashes might have been anticipated. But there were two possible exceptions to this general tolerance: monotheistic religions, such as Judaism and Christianity, which would not subscribe to the principle, 'If we accept your gods we expect you to accept ours'; or religions which involved cults tending to cause popular disorders or gross practices, or which had political implications. In the case of Druidism the Romans disapproved of their practice of human sacrifice, and also feared the unifying influence which their beliefs exercised upon native resistance in both Gaul and Britain. For these reasons the emperor Claudius decreed the complete suppression of Druidism, a policy which reached its fulfilment when Suetonius Paulinus finally destroyed the Druids' sacred groves in Anglesey and eliminated their priesthood. But apart from this ruthless action, Roman religious policy in Britain was 'live and let live', which resulted in a considerable degree of assimilation of Celtic and Roman cults.

But Roman disapproval of one aspect of Celtic religion was reciprocated by Celtic dislike of one Roman cult in particular, that of the emperor. This practice developed slowly, for although the deranged Caligula demanded to be worshipped as a god, other early emperors made more modest claims. They might become gods after death, but in this life any worship accorded to them must be limited: thus Claudius deprecated an offer of a temple to himself by the Alexandrians: 'since I do not wish to seem vulgar . . . and I judge that temples have been set apart by all ages for the gods alone . . .' However, it was clear that if the loyalty of scattered tribes could be focused on a common ruler, then a greater sense of unity might be created among them, and so in Gaul an altar to 'the goddess Roma and Augustus' had been set up

The temple of Claudius at Colchester, centre of the imperial cult in Britain. A reconstruction.

in Lyons to form the centre for an imperial cult and a provincial assembly. In Britain Colchester had hardly been captured before an altar and temple were established there as a centre for the imperial cult. Possibly the dedication was at first only to the 'spirit' (*numen*) of the emperor, and not until the temple was rebuilt after its destruction by Boudicca was it dedicated to 'the god Claudius' since he was now dead and enrolled among the gods (*Divus*). At all events, its original construction, which involved the Britons in considerable expense and labour, was an affront to their independence, and it became the symbol of their subjection and the target of their indignation ('The citadel of everlasting domination'): hence its destruction. But over the years relations gradually changed, and as peace returned and reconciliation to Roman rule increased, this centre of the imperial cult became the focus of imperial loyalty instead of hatred. A provincial council, formed by representative leaders of the various *civitates*, gathered together here each year to celebrate the cult of the emperor and to discuss matters of mutual interest under the presidency of the annually elected chief priest of the cult. The council also served as a kind of safety-valve since it could make representations direct to the emperor in Rome about the governor and provincial affairs. The centre was possibly later moved to London, but more probably remained at Colchester.

Besides this centralized worship, the imperial cult was also celebrated in the four Roman colonies, in each of which six priests, *seviri Augustales*, were appointed from the wealthy freedmen to maintain the cult at their own expense. An inscription of M. Aurelius Lunaris records that he was in fact *sevir Augustalis* at both York and Lincoln. Furthermore, the inhabitants of Britain had an increasing, if indirect, interest in the continued welfare of the Roman state, so that many dedications begin to appear to the spirit or power of the emperor or emperors (*numen Augusti*), either individually or in association with other gods. Honours were also paid to members of the imperial household. A magistrate of Brough (Petuaria) dedicated a new theatre stage 'in honour of the emperor Antoninus Pius and to the imperial spirits' (*numinibus Augustorum*), while at Colchester a dedication was made to the imperial spirits and the god Mercury. An early example of similar intent is the famous inscription already mentioned of Cogidubnus, which records the dedication of a temple to Neptune and Minerva on behalf of the safety of the divine (i.e. imperial) house by the guild of smiths and its members. The inhabitants could also show their loyalty by making vows for the emperor's safety or by erecting statues in his honour. A large bronze head of Claudius recovered from the river Alde (see p. 38) came from a statue other than that found in the temple; a fragment of a pre-Hadrianic imperial statue was found at Silchester, and a large bronze head of Hadrian (see p. 59) came from London. Suetonius records that there were numerous statues and busts of the emperor Titus in Britain, where he had served as a military tribune during his earlier career.

Worship of the emperor was complemented by worship of the deities of the Roman state, at first mainly by the soldiers (the army had an official calendar of religious festivals), or by Roman citizens living in the four colonies. But the practice gradually spread, particularly after AD 212, when all the provincials had become Roman citizens. Chief among these deities was the Capitoline triad of Jupiter, Juno and Minerva, whose joint worship went back to the very beginnings of the Roman republic, when the great temple on the Capitol at Rome was dedicated to Jupiter Optimus Maximus. A smaller version of this *capitolium* must have existed in the *coloniae* and the *municipia*, and each year on 3 January the commanding officer of the military forts dedicated a new altar to Jupiter Optimus Maximus, the existing one being buried on the edge of the parade ground. At Maryport, Cumbria, an inscription records: 'To Jupiter, Best and Greatest [*Optimus Maximus*], the First Cohort of Spaniards, which is commanded by M. Maenius Agrippa, tribune, set up this altar.' Similarly, at Newstead (Trimontium) on the Tweed, C. Arrius Domitianus, centurion of Legio XX Valeria Victrix, 'Gladly, willingly and duly' paid his vow to Jupiter Optimus Maximus. Other Roman gods to receive dedications included Mars, Neptune, Apollo, Vulcan, Ceres and Mercury, and their cults would have involved the appointment of local Roman citizens as priests (*flamines*).

Such dedications are naturally found most frequently in military areas: at Housesteads Mars was honoured by Q. Florus Maternus, officer commanding the First Tungrian Cohort, and Hercules by the same cohort under the command of P. Aelius Modestus. Another dedication to Hercules was made by P. Sextianus, a prefect from Xanten, 'after the slaughter of a band of barbarians by the Cavalry Regiment called Augusta for valour'.

Neptune received the attention not only of Cogidubnus and, not unnaturally, of a commander of the British fleet, the *classis Britannica*, L. Aufidius Pantera in the time of Hadrian, but also of Legio VI Victrix when it arrived from the Rhineland by sea at Tynemouth in AD 122. An altar, decorated with a dolphin and trident, has been found deep in the mud of the river's mouth, perhaps deliberately sunk by the dedicators. A legionary centurion at Newstead made a dedication to Apollo. The villagers (*vicani*) of

Sculptured head of Mars, found in Upper Thames Street, London, 1975.

Vindolanda paid a vow by dedicating an altar to Vulcan for the imperial house and the spirits of the Augusti (*pro domu divina et numinibus Augustorum*). Our knowledge of these Roman deities is not confined to inscriptions: a very considerable number of sculptures also survive, both in stone and bronze, in the round and in relief. Thus a monument in London displayed the figures of several Roman deities: in 1975, in Upper Thames Street, 52 sculptured stones were found which had been re-used to build a wall. They include the damaged heads of Venus and Mars, and the legs of Vulcan and Minerva. Occasionally statue and inscription were combined, as on a bronze statuette of Mars from Foss Dike in Lincolnshire where we read, 'To the god Mars and the spirits of the emperors, the Colasuni, Bruccius and Caratius, presented this at their own expense at the cost of 100 sesterces; Celatus the coppersmith made it and gave a pound of bronze made at the cost of three denarii.'

The Romans also worshipped a great number of personifications, such as Victoria and Abundantia. Thus at Rough Castle near Falkirk, the Sixth Nervian Cohort, acting under the command of Flavius Betto, centurion of Legio XX Valeria Victrix, erected an altar to Victoria, while the success achieved by Septimius Severus was celebrated when the people of Gigthis in Severus' native Africa recalled 'the British Victory of our three emperors', namely Severus, Caracalla and Geta. Districts also could be personified, as when a centurion at York made a dedication to the Heavenly Spirit of Brigantia (*Caelesti Brigantiae*) as well as to Jupiter Dolichenus, the Eternal, and to Safety (*Salus*). Personifications of localities or groups of human beings, namely Genii, as indeed of vaguer concepts such as Fortuna and Abundantia, are, like the more anthropomorphic deities, also found in sculptured form.

ROMANO-CELTIC DEITIES

Since Roman and Celtic gods were increasingly worshipped side by side, it was natural that when their attributes or functions appeared not dissimilar they should become assimilated and receive a double name. Thus while many Roman deities remained exclusively Roman, some, including Mars in particular, were merged so that a degree of syncretism was achieved by the so-called *interpretatio Romana*. This process started as early as the time of Julius Caesar, who claimed that the Celts of Gaul worshipped Mercury and had numerous images of him; they recognized him as the inventor of arts, the guide of travellers and the adviser in money-making and commerce. After

The Celtic Genii Cucullati, 'hooded godlets of healing, fertility and after-life', from a domestic shrine in the *vicus* of Housesteads fort on the Wall.

him came Apollo, Mars, Jupiter and Minerva. Whether in individual cases the initiative to identify similar deities came from the Celts or the Romans, any assimilation was only very approximate, and we need not assume close resemblances: the two gods compared merely shared some common attributes. The Cumbrian god Cocidius, for instance, was identified with both Mars and Silvanus; Maponus (cf. Mabon of the Welsh *Mabinogion*) with Apollo; and Sulis (the deity of Bath) with Minerva. We find detachments of soldiers on Hadrian's Wall making dedications to Mars Cocidius as well as separately to 'the god Cocidius' and 'the god Mars'. Others identified Mars with a native deity Thincsus: a formation of Frisians at Housesteads made a dedication 'to the god Mars Thincsus, and the two Alaisiagae, and to the *numen* of the emperor'. Mars was also equated with other native deities, namely Medocius (from the Lowlands?), Belatucadrus from the north of England, and Ocelus and Lenus, both at Caerwent. Mercury appears once, at Colchester, as Mercurius Andescocis, and Apollo as Apollo Anextiomarus.

Even when identifications were not achieved, Roman influences hastened the development of Celtic deities into more specific form, with dedicatory

The goddess Brigantia, a regional north British deity here endowed with Oriental and classical attributes, perhaps in honour of the emperor Septimius Severus.

inscriptions written in Latin. These dedications are particularly numerous in the district of Hadrian's Wall, where they reveal the cults of such deities as Cocidius, Maponus, Belatucadrus, Vitris (or Huitris), Antenociticus, as well as the water nymph Coventina. Sculptured reliefs depict the Celtic mother-goddesses, and the attractive little deities in hooded cloaks called the Genii Cucullati.

Sulis, the Celtic water goddess, is known only at Bath, but Nodens appears both in Lancashire and at Lydney in Gloucestershire, where his temple became the centre of a healing cult. This sanctuary, with its adjacent buildings, was a late construction (after AD 364) built on a hill overlooking the Severn estuary, and it is interesting not only for its original activities but also for some of the objects it has yielded up, especially two bronzes and an inscription. These are a fine bronze statuette of an Irish wolfhound and a bronze ritual diadem, depicting a god driving a four-horse chariot (the classical sun god, here perhaps depicted as a river deity with its accompanying tritons and anchor). In addition to a dedication to 'Mars Nodens', we have a lead plaque which contains a curse: 'To the god Nodens: Silvianus has lost his ring. He has dedicated [its value] to Nodens. Among those who are called Senicianus do not allow health until he brings it to the temple of Nodens.' Silvianus evidently feared to accuse a certain Senicianus by name, but made this oblique charge which involved Nodens, a god who could give (or, as Silvianus hoped, withhold) health. It is a moot point whether this Senicianus is to be identified with the 'owner' of a fine gold ring found near Silchester depicting the head of Venus and inscribed with a Christian formula, 'Senicianus, may you live in God'.

Less religious than superstitious was the Roman habit of cursing one's enemy by writing his name on a piece of lead and fixing the tablet with a nail, often to a tomb. In primitive use man and name are one, so that the victim became a victim of the gods of the underworld. Besides Silvianus' curse, other examples are found in Roman Britain. One from London reads simply: 'Titus Egnatius Tyranus is "fixed" [*defictus est*] and P. Cicereius is fixed.' More detail and venom is contained in a second example set out in crude cursive writing and pierced by seven nails: 'I fix Tertia Maria and her life and mind and memory and liver and lungs mixed, fate, thoughts, memory; so may she not be able to speak secrets nor . . .' Time, if not this curse, has in fact preserved her secrets inviolate. In 1977 no less than 162 tightly rolled lead scrolls were found at a temple site of the mid-fourth century at Uley in Gloucestershire; they were probably originally fixed to the temple walls. The process of unrolling them has not yet been completed, but many, if not most, contain curses, thus witnessing to the widespread nature of the practice.

The classical type of temple, with columns, pediment and high podium, is rare in Roman Britain, as we have seen. It made its first appearance in the early days of conquest with the construction of Claudius' temple at Colchester, and doubtless others were built in the four *coloniae*. Although little survives of the structure of the temple at Bath, the remains of its pediment, with the famous head of Sulis show that it was in classical form. The temple at Wroxeter has classical features. Here the rectangular temple building (*cella*) was raised on a podium, with a flight of steps in front, its columns topped with Corinthian capitals. It was enclosed by a rectangular courtyard which was entered through a portico of six columns. This temple connects with the Romano-Celtic type with its double rectangular box, one within the other, the outer portico or cloister rising up to enclose the inner shrine (see page 100).

The ancestry of the Romano-Celtic temple is uncertain. Since the Celts carried out their ritual practices in natural surroundings such as groves or beside sacred springs, they appear not to have needed temples. However, some rectangular earthworks of the first century BC, which are found more widely in continental Europe but do occur in Britain, e.g. at Ashill in Norfolk, have been thought to be sanctuaries, and might therefore have contributed to the development of the Romano-Celtic temple. But this is far from certain. It seems more likely that the structure developed in central and eastern France about the beginning of the first century BC and spread to Britain not long before the conquest, though of course some of these buildings, especially those in the country as opposed to the town, may have been developed on the sites of earlier Iron Age shrines. At any rate, the growth and spread of these buildings in Britain occurred very largely under

Coventina, a British water goddess, was worshipped at a well in Carrawburgh on the Wall, where this relief was set up.

Roman rule. Variations of pattern are found, the central shrine sometimes being polygonal (as at Caerwent and at Pagans Hill in Somerset) or perhaps even circular (Lullingstone?). The temples were often surrounded by a rectangular enclosure (*temenos*) which might take the form of a ditch or wall of greater or lesser elaboration, designed to delimit the holy ground. The size also varied considerably. At festival time the large temples, which were intended for congregational rather than intra-mural worship, would be thronged by crowds of participants. Smaller local shrines also continued to attract a following. For example, at Carrawburgh the devout (or superstitious) for generations went on throwing coins – some 16,000 survive – as well as more costly offerings into the spring of the water-nymph Coventina, whose shrine was somewhat unorthodox in that it contained a well in place of the *cella*. Coventina also won the devotion of soldiers on the neighbouring Wall. A relief which depicts the water goddess herself, reclining on a water-lily leaf, was dedicated by Titus Domitius Cosconianus, prefect of the First Batavian Cohort.

The Romans introduced into Britain not only many of their native deities but also some Oriental mystery cults. Since many of these offered a hope of personal immortality and involved the individual initiation of each worshipper, they had a greater appeal for many than some of the more formalized state cults. Consequently, from the early days of the empire they increasingly spread westwards and finally reached Britain through the participation of soldiers and merchants.

Mithraism derived from the worship of the Persian god Mithras, a god of light and truth, but as his cult spread westwards it assumed new features. In order to achieve personal courage and a high standard of conduct, the initiates had to undergo various tests and ordeals, including a symbolic burial, before they could be reborn into the faith. The rites and worship were celebrated in small oblong temples, sometimes constructed partly underground, to resemble the cave in which Mithras was said to have sacrificed a sacred bull. The worshippers reclined on benches along the two sides for a sacred meal, while at the end was a statue of Mithras sacrificing the bull and accompanied by two torch-bearers, as well as altars and reliefs

Mithras the Bull-slayer, from the site of the Walbrook Mithraeum, London. Late second or third century AD.

dedicated by the members. Pine cones provided incense, and a well water for ritual purposes. Various episodes in the god's legendary life were depicted in sculpture or painting, while fragments of painted hymns have also been found. The initiates were classed in seven grades: the Raven, Bride, Soldier, Lion, Persian, Messenger of the Sun, and Father. Perhaps dressed in the trappings of these grades, a small group of men (women were excluded from the cult) would gather in these dark 'caves' in a ceremony which might culminate in the sacrifice of a bull which shed life-giving blood. At a crucial moment, Mithras' sunray crown might suddenly blaze with light, as shown for instance by a 'halo', pierced for illumination, depicted on an altar found at the Mithraeum at Carrawburgh. Mithras was closely linked with the sun, and is sometimes described in inscriptions as 'the Unconquered Sun, Mithras' (*Sol invictus Mithras*).

The rigorous demands of the Mithraic initiation and way of life limited the extension of the cult, and remains of only five temples survive in Britain, though evidence suggests their possible existence elsewhere, e.g. at York, Caerleon, Chester, Carlisle and High Rochester. Four of the five surviving Mithraea lie close to forts, at Carrawburgh, Housesteads, Rudchester and Caernarvon, and were built about AD 200 or soon afterwards. The largest, at Rudchester, measured only 26 feet by 60 feet; the smallest, at Carrawburgh, could hold only about 12 men. In contrast, the rich temple discovered in 1954 in the London Walbrook, was 60 feet by 25 feet, excluding the narthex. This was first built in the second half of the second century, and

The little temple of Mithras at Carrawburgh, founded soon after AD 205 and finally desecrated in the fourth century.

remained in use until after the mid-fourth century. It contained a number of works of art which had been deliberately buried in ancient times, including marble heads of Mithras, Minerva and Serapis, a large hand of Mithras in the act of slaying the bull, a seated Mercury, and a Bacchic group, together with a richly adorned silver casket. In general, the evidence suggests that the cult made its primary appeal to the merchants of a cosmopolitan city like London and to the upper ranks of the army, since most of the dedications in the Mithraea on the Wall were made by senior officers.

Another mystery cult, that of the mother goddess Cybele from Asia Minor, was very different, being characterized by ecstatic frenzies, eunuch priests, fasting, purification, the sacrifice of a bull whose blood (unlike at the Mithraic tauroctony) flowed down on to a priest or worshipper placed below, the carrying of the bull's genitals in a special vessel, and a descent into an underground cave for the performance of other rites. Cybele seems to have had a temple in London, to judge from the discovery of a castration clasp decorated with her bust, and two statues of her consort Atys. Although a few statues and dedications do not necessarily entail the existence of a temple, they suggest the possibility of other temples at Gloucester and certain places on Hadrian's Wall. But on the whole, the worship of Cybele in Britain does not appear to have been widespread.

Very different again was the worship of the Egyptian goddess Isis, which also involved individual initiation (for both men and women) as well as an elaborate cult drama celebrating the myth of Osiris. Iron rattles (*sistra*), which were used in her worship, and a steelyard weight in the form of a bust of the goddess, have been found in London, but until recently the only direct evidence for a temple in Britain was a jug from London, inscribed *Londini ad fanum Isidis* ('London; next to the temple of Isis'); this surprisingly is as early as the third quarter of the first century. However, among the sculptured stones found in 1975 in Upper Thames Street were altars to Jupiter Optimus Maximus and to Isis. The latter was dedicated, probably in the third century, by Marcus Martianius, governor of the Augusti (probably of Britannia Superior), who in honour of the imperial house ordered the restoration of the temple of Isis (*templum Isidis*), which had collapsed through old age. Closely associated with Isis was the god Serapis, for whom a temple was built early in the third century at York by the commander of Legio VI Victrix, as recorded in an inscription. But since a head of Serapis was found in the London Mithraeum, the discovery of heads elsewhere (e.g. Colchester) does not necessarily imply the existence of temples, but only of interest.

Other Eastern deities whose worship spread to Britain include Dolichenus, a local sky god of Commagene, commemorated from the mid-second century by many altars. He was identified with Jupiter, and his consort Caelestis with Juno Regina, the cult reaching its greatest popularity when the emperor Alexander Severus (225–35) and the empress-mother Julia Mammaea were associated with these deities and worshipped accordingly. A stone statuette of Juno Regina has been found in the regimental headquarters at Chesters. From Syria came the great Baal of Heliopolis, identified as Jupiter Heliopolitanus; the Unconquered Sun (*Sol invictus*), often associated with Mithras; a mother goddess who personified

Syria, known from a metrical hymn at Carvoran (on the Wall), where Dea Syria is to be equated with Julia Domna; Baal's consort Astarte, and Hercules (Melkart) from Tyre. These last two received offerings at Corbridge, probably in connection with Eastern traders, with inscriptions in Greek: 'Thou seest me, an altar of Astarte: Pulcher set me up', and 'To Tyrian Hercules, Diodora the High-Priestess'.

CHRISTIANITY

Britain was little affected by the early growth of Christianity as it gradually gathered strength during the first two centuries AD despite intermittent persecution. By 200 it was becoming one of the major religions of the Graeco-Roman world, but the refusal of Christians to accept the gods of Rome or to participate in the imperial cult rendered it more vulnerable whenever increasing national difficulties and disasters required a scapegoat. So periods of partial toleration by the Roman state were followed by sharp bouts of persecution in 202 under Septimius Severus, in 250 under Decius, and in 258 under Valerian. These culminated in the 'Great Persecution' started by Diocletian in 303, which was finally brought to an end by the emperor Constantine's conversion. Thus Christianity triumphed, and when the emperor presided at the Council of Nicaea in 325 it had in fact become the religion of the empire. Paganism began to decline until finally, in 391, Theodosius closed the temples and banned all forms of pagan worship.

The arrival of Christianity in Britain remains obscure. Whether the legends of visits by St Peter and by Joseph of Arimathaea can legitimately be used to suggest an early date remains very doubtful. Tertullian, writing in about AD 206, says that 'parts of Britain inaccessible to the Romans have been subjected to Christ': presumably parts of Scotland or even Ireland. Origen, writing a few years later, asks: 'when ever did the land of Britain agree on the worship of one god before the arrival of Christ?' Bede records the stories of three British martyrs under Diocletian's persecution: Aaron and Iulius of Caerleon, and Alban of Verulamium. There are no good grounds for rejecting the basic facts, though a case has been advanced for dating the martyrdoms to 208–9 rather than to Diocletian's persecution, since Augustine stated that the western parts of the empire, ruled by the Caesar Constantius, did not suffer persecution at that time. But this statement is not beyond question. The names of three British bishops – from York, London and probably Lincoln – who attended the council convened by Constantine of Arles in 314, are recorded. British bishops also attended the Council of Ariminum (Rimini) in 359, and three of these accepted the emperor's offer of free transport through lack of private means (*inopia proprii*). Their action, however, does not necessarily prove widespread poverty in the British churches: these three bishops may have embraced personal poverty on religious grounds, or they may have accepted the subvention because (as the historian Sulpicius Severus says) they considered it 'more holy to burden the Treasury than individuals', i.e. presumably their own flocks (*Sanctius putantes fiscum gravare quam singulos*). Thus the literary evidence, such as it is, points to a fully organized and active church in the early fourth century.

Head of Serapis from the Walbrook Mithraeum, London. Late second century AD.

The archaeological evidence is also far from prolific, and inscriptions are not numerous. This fact is not really surprising: Christianity is likely to have spread first among the poorer inhabitants of town and countryside, and, in any case, inscriptions of all kinds of the fourth century are few compared with those of the two previous centuries. Christianity appears to have remained socially and economically obscure for a long time, gradually penetrating somewhat further up the social scale, until it finally blazes into prominence for us with the magnificent silver tableware and mosaics belonging to Christian owners of some of the later villas.

Christian symbols and phrases survive on a number of objects, especially the Chi-Rho monogram (the first two letters of the name of Christ in Greek), the letters Alpha and Omega, and phrases such as 'Hope in God' (*Spes in Deo*), or 'Live in God' (*Vivas in Deo*). A copy of the cryptic word-square (Rotas/Opera/Tenet/Arepo/Sator), which is found widely in the Roman world as far east as the Euphrates, was painted on a wall at Cirencester (in the second or third century?). This is probably, though not quite certainly, a Christian cryptogram, making two anagrams of Pater Noster and Alpha and Omega; if so, it was a secret sign of recognition between Christians, and may have continued as a general symbol of the faith after the persecution had ended at the start of the fourth century. And part of another copy, possibly the earliest archaeological evidence of Christianity in Britain, was found in 1978 on a piece of pottery at Manchester, dating to AD 175–80. Chi-Rho is found on some pewter bowls, and also (together with Alpha and Omega) on a large lead tank from Suffolk. Whether these vessels were used for religious purposes is uncertain, especially as a fourth-century metal-dealer named Syagrius stamped several ingots of pewter with these

Romano-British Christianity: a silver strainer with Chi-Rho monogram on the handle, found at Water Newton, dating to the fourth century.

letters, together with his name and *Spes in Deo*; they were found in the Thames near Battersea. Finally, there is the magnificent hoard of silver objects of the fourth century found in 1975 at Water Newton in Huntingdonshire. Many of the objects, bowls, cups and small triangular plaques bear the Chi-Rho monogram, and one bowl is inscribed, 'I, Publianus, honour your sacred shrine [*sanctum altare tuum*], trusting in you, O Lord.' The reasons for the burial of this rich collection are uncertain, whether raids from overseas, unrest in Britain, or fear of persecution.

Christian services were at first held in private houses, and this practice probably continued at least till the time of Constantine. But public or semi-public places of worship gradually became available, and churches were built in some of the towns. Literary sources imply the existence of several, e.g. at Canterbury and St Albans, while the bishops already mentioned also presumably had churches. However, buildings which were almost certainly used for Christian worship survive only at Silchester and Lullingstone, though an unexplained structure at Richborough has recently been identified as a Christian church of *c.* AD 400. At Silchester a small apsidal building, 42 feet long, with aisles and wings, was definitely designed for religious, and most probably for Christian, use. The apse was in the west, but this is common in fourth-century Christian churches in Italy and North Africa.

The Lullingstone villa was partly reconstructed *c.* 350–60 so as to cut off four interconnecting rooms, and the walls of two of these were decorated with Christian subjects. In the main room, between the seven columns of a painted colonnade, are human figures, and at least three of these hold their arms and hands outstretched sideways in the typical attitude of an *orans*, an early Christian at prayer (as often depicted in the catacombs in Rome). They probably represent the family, one figure being that of a dead member, and another seated figure probably the paterfamilias. On another wall was a large wreath containing a red Chi-Rho, and traces of a landscape with a Christian scene. The wall of another room also had a Chi-Rho wreath, as did the antechamber with the addition of an Alpha and Omega. Since the complex was cut off from the rest of the villa, it was most probably designed as a house-church for the public. It may have continued in use longer than the villa itself, until destroyed by fire *c.* 400.

Christian worship in villas is also shown by the floor mosaics at Frampton and Hinton St Mary in Dorset. Their mythological scenes interestingly illustrate the continuity of pagan motives, adapted symbolically to Christian use: thus Orpheus playing to the animals is equated with the Good Shepherd. At Frampton, figures of Cupid and Neptune share the scene with a Chi-Rho monogram. The floor at Hinton St Mary, found in 1963, shows Bellerophon attacking the Chimera; on the central roundel the bust of a beardless man with fair hair, the Chi-Rho monogram behind his head, is almost certainly a representation of Christ; possibly Bellerophon is symbolically depicted defeating sin and death. Since the decoration of these two villas is less specifically Christian than that of Lullingstone, it may be that the rooms were not house-chapels but only owned by Christians.

Even after the official adoption of Christianity by Rome, a long struggle with paganism continued, especially in the countryside. This received brief

The earliest known British depiction of Christ: fourth-century mosaic from Hinton St Mary, Dorset, now at the British Museum.

encouragement during the pagan reaction of the emperor Julian (361–3) and is marked by the building or renewal of some temples, including the great temple of Nodens at Lydney. Here the ground-plan, dated to the second half of the fourth century, appears to some to have been influenced by the arrangement of Christian churches. Another more typically Romano-Celtic temple is found in the middle of the old hillfort at Maiden Castle, and the *temenos* wall of a temple at Verulamium was also rebuilt. It was in Julian's reign that a governor of part of Britain (Prima) restored a pagan 'giant-column' erected in honour of Jupiter at Cirencester. Indeed, despite the edicts of the emperors Gratian (382) and Theodosius (391) to close all temples and to ban all pagan cults, from Julian's time until the early fifth century there was something of a pagan revival in the countryside of Britain, which was conveniently far away from the central authority. However, the temples gradually declined, first in the towns and then in the country. This process was probably accelerated in some places, e.g. Silchester and the London Mithraeum, through destruction by zealous local Christians, and in others by barbarian attacks, but the chief cause, especially in the country, was more often neglect and decay. Nor were they later taken over as holy places by the Saxons, who did, however, occasionally use them as cemeteries.

As Christianity began to take deeper root in Britain, it was faced with challenges from within as well as from without. Pelagius, a Briton, preached a heretical doctrine which denied Original Sin and the necessity for Divine Grace, and emphasized free will and moral effort. Pelagius' travels to Rome, Africa and Palestine would have reminded a wider world of the existence of British Christianity, though theologically he was defeated, not least through the efforts of Augustine. But his views were so disturbing to orthodox British Christians that in 429, soon after his death, they appealed to the Church in Gaul which sent St Germanus of Auxerre to preach the true faith in British churches and countryside. He also helped in another sphere: before becoming a bishop he had been a distinguished soldier, and was able to lead a local militia to victory against an attack of Picts and Saxons in a battle where he gave his troops the war-cry of 'Alleluia'. The Church in Britain also began to display a more active missionary zeal, as shown by the work of Ninian in Scotland and of Patrick in Ireland. However, when the Saxons stormed their way in with fire and sword during the second half of the fifth century, the Celtic Church in England, together with the rest of Celtic culture, was submerged. It disappeared in the towns, and where it survived in the highland zone its members were cut off from contact with Rome and the Continent. It was a distinctive legacy from Roman Britain, so distinctive that it found difficulty in coming to terms with the Roman Church when, in 597, St Augustine arrived in Kent to convert the Saxons: not all differences between these two branches of the Church were eliminated even by the Synod of Whitby in 664.

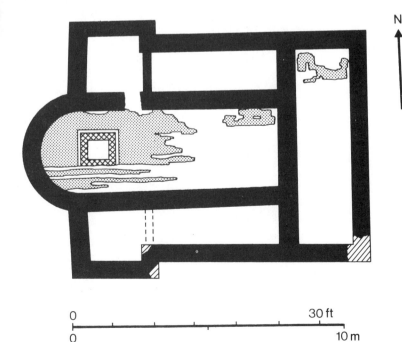

N

Plan of the tiny (42 × 24 feet) Christian church at Silchester, oriented east–west, and showing traces of tessellated pavement, with a square pattern in mosaic at the base of the apse.

0   30 ft

0   10 m

10

The end of Roman Britain

THE FOURTH CENTURY

By warfare and reconstruction Constantius and his son Constantine had laid the foundations for half a century of prosperity in Britain. This had been made possible only by the far-reaching reforms which Diocletian and Constantine had applied to the whole empire, thereby saving it from complete dissolution and disaster. Both civil service and army were radically reformed, with a clear separation between civilian and military powers. For the purposes of civil administration Diocletian divided the empire into twelve districts called dioceses, each governed by a *vicarius*, who was technically a deputy of one of the praetorian prefects.

Britain formed one of these dioceses, and its *vicarius*, who was based on London, was responsible in the first instance to the praetorian prefect of Gaul, residing at Trier and administering Gaul, Britain and Spain. At the same time the number of provinces was greatly increased by the subdivision of existing units. Britain was divided into four: Britannia Prima, Britannia Secunda, Maxima Caesariensis (probably named after Maximianus, Constantine's father-in-law) and Flavia Caesariensis (after Flavius Constantius). The governors, called *praesides*, had civil but not military authority.

The areas of the provinces are uncertain: Maxima was in the south, with its centre at London, temporarily renamed Caesarea and later Augusta; Prima was in the west, including Wales, with its capital at Cirencester; Secunda was in the north, possibly with York as the capital; and in the east Flavia's capital may have been Lincoln. In 369 a fifth province, Valentia (named in honour of the reigning emperors, Valentinian and Valens) was established under a consular governor, and probably located in northern England with its capital at Carlisle.

The Roman army was divided into a central mobile field force (*comitatenses*) commanded by *magistri militum*, and stationary frontier garrisons (*limitanei*) commanded by *duces*. The *Notitia Dignitatum*, compiled about AD 395 and containing lists of the officials of the whole empire, records three commands in Britain: the *Dux Britanniarum*, with headquarters at York, in charge of the frontier area; the *Comes Litoris Saxonici*, in command of coastal forts; and the *Comes Britanniarum*, in command of the field army. The Duke may have taken over military duties in the north as early as Diocletian, and the Count of the Saxon Shore is attested in 367 but may go back to Constantine. The office of the Count of Britain appears as a temporary appointment before the middle of the fourth century, and only became permanent for a brief period in the late fourth or early fifth century (perhaps in

Opposite, Saxon Shore forts in the beleaguered British province are illustrated in the fifth-century *Notitia Dignitatum*, a late-empire administrative document.

402; the date of 410, which would imply a reoccupation of Britain after the withdrawal, need not be accepted). These Counts and Dukes were soldiers without experience of civil administration. Selected from the officers of the auxiliary regiments, they were often uneducated and of barbarian rather than Roman stock, as shown by names like Fullofaudes, Duke of Britain.

Helped by this division between civil and military authority, Britain enjoyed a long period of comparative peace and quiet prosperity in town and country. For several decades little is recorded, and 'happy the country that has no history'. However, the tide of troubles began to rise once again as the Picts of central Scotland (a name by now applied to a fusion of Caledonians with other tribes) and the Scots from Ireland moved to the attack. In 343 the emperor Constans thought it necessary to visit Britain, and even to cross the Channel in midwinter, an unusual risk which was commemorated by a large bronze medal referring to his embarking at Boulogne (Bononia Oceanensis). He appears to have stabilized the position on the Wall and reorganized the frontier scouts (*areani*) who since Caracalla's time had operated beyond it. The outposts at High Rochester, Risingham and Bewcastle had been attacked about this time, and the first was apparently now abandoned, while the friendly Votadini were given a greater share in the defence. The fort at Pevensey was added to those of the Saxon Shore about now, and Constans may have taken this step against increasing Saxon raids. The office of Count of the Saxon Shore will have been instituted at this time, if not earlier.

Bronze coin (AD 350–3) of Magnentius, a British native who seized power in the mid-fourth century.

When Magnentius, a man of British origin, made a successful bid for the throne, Britain was not seriously affected except that the usurper denuded her of more troops for his campaigns on the Continent (350–53). After his defeat, Constantius II sent a notorious police agent, Paul the Notary, to root out Magnentius' surviving supporters in Britain. When Martinus, the popular *vicarius* of Britain, boldly tried to withstand Paul's inquisition, he was forced to commit suicide.

The storm was gathering fast. The emperor Julian, who had transported much grain from Britain, heard that the Picts and Scots were again ravaging territory along the Wall, and so in 360 he sent a field force under his *magister militum*, Lupicinus, who took some holding action. But the tempest broke in 367 when Britain was invaded by a 'conspiracy' of Picts, Scots and Attacotti (Irish?) in the north, and Saxons and Franks on the coasts. The frontier *areani*, who should have given warning in the north, had collaborated with the Picts. The Wall was overrun, Nectaridus, Count of the Saxon Shore was killed, and Fullofaudes, Duke of Britain, was overwhelmed. Army discipline collapsed, soldiers deserted, slaves escaped, disorder reigned. The emperor Valentinian was too busy campaigning against the Alemanni to come himself, but he sent Count Theodosius (*Comes rei militaris*) with a field army of four regiments.

Theodosius, who had to start clearing up as far south as London, appointed a new Count of Britain and a new *vicarius*. By 369 he had driven out the invaders and restored order. He then carried out a major work of reconstruction, though lack of precise archaeological evidence often leaves details obscure. Neither towns nor villas appear to have suffered extensive damage, but Theodosius is said by the historian Ammianus Marcellinus to have helped the former, probably refortifying them with towers for *ballistae* (see p. 96), and possibly stationing small detachments of soldiers in some. In Wales many forts, such as Caerhun, were held; some (e.g. Caernarvon) rebuilt, and a base for the fleet was established at Holyhead against the Irish. More important was the north, where curiously the Wall had also escaped major damage: probably the Picts had bypassed it by sea. At any rate, Theodosius built some lookout posts on the Yorkshire coast to guard against the recurrence of such amphibious operations. The Wall was, nevertheless, strengthened by some repairs and rebuilding, the labour perhaps being supplied by towns further south – if some building inscriptions are to be dated to this time: thus a building stone at Carvoran records, 'The *Civitas* of the Dumnonii built this.' The outlying forts were abandoned, and the system of *areani* abolished, but it is very far from certain that *vici* on the Wall were also abandoned and the civilians moved into the forts. Also controversial is the status of some kings in the Lowlands of Scotland who had Roman names, such as Cluim (Clemens), Cinhil (Quintilius), Annwn (Antonius), and Padarn (Paternus). Since Padarn was also called Pesrut (the Man of the Red Cloak) some scholars suppose that these kings were set up by Rome as buffer rulers between the Picts and the Wall; others, in view of the lack of any Roman pottery in this area, suggest that they were anti-Roman and owed their Roman names merely to conversion to Christianity. But, whatever the details, Theodosius' work of reconstruction was widespread and effective, as

The great usurper: gold *solidus*, minted at London, showing the head of Magnus Maximus, the British general recorded in Welsh literature as Macsen Wledig.

shown by the prosperity enjoyed by both towns and villas during the next quarter of a century.

If the south enjoyed a respite, the north was again threatened in 382 by Picts and Scots who were thrown back by Magnus Maximus, probably *Dux Britanniarum*, a general who had served under Theodosius. However, the old story repeated itself: Maximus was elected emperor by the army in Britain (he reappears later in Welsh legend as Macsen Wledig) and took many troops to fight on the Continent where he overthrew the emperor Gratian and retained power in the west until 388. This weakening of the army did not, as was generally believed until fairly recently, lead to the final evacuation of Hadrian's Wall in 383. Its continuing occupation is attested by a few later coins and probably by the quantity of pottery (although this is difficult to date precisely). The garrison presumably declined sharply in numbers and military efficiency, but some soldiers and civilians still stayed on in the forts and *vici*: after all, the soldiers were mostly 'natives', men who had been recruited locally. However, western Britain was in danger after the withdrawal of Legio XX from Chester and the abandonment of the fort at Caernarvon (though the discovery of two Theodosian coins suggests the continuance of some garrison for a while after 383). Irish tribes attacked before the end of the century: Scots began to settle in the Lleyn peninsula in the north, the Deisi in southwest Wales.

Seaborne invasions continued, but were checked temporarily when Stilicho, the Vandal general who was acting as regent for the young emperor

Honorius, sent an expedition against them in 396–8. This, though successful, was probably less enduring than is implied in the poem of Claudian, who puts into the mouth of Britannia the claim, 'Stilicho gave me aid when I was at the mercy of neighbouring tribes, when the Scots raised all Hibernia against me, and the sea foamed with hostile oars. Thanks to his care, I need not fear the weapons of the Scots or tremble at the Pict, or keep watch along my shores for the Saxon who would come whatever wind might blow.' The only apparent support thought to be given by archaeology to such flattery was a single inscription from Pevensey (HON. AUG. ANDRIA) which suggested some strengthening of at least one fort of the Saxon Shore. Unfortunately, however, this has recently been shown to be a modern forgery.

THE LAST STAGES AND 'SUB-ROMAN' BRITAIN

The whole Roman world was now increasingly threatened by the peoples breaking through the frontiers. In 395 the empire was formally split into two parts, East and West. Alaric, the Visigoth leader, was on the warpath; he appeared in Italy in 401, and from 408 besieged Rome itself three times until he finally entered it in 410. To meet this challenge Stilicho had been forced to withdraw more troops from Britain. Vandals, Alans, Suevi and Burgundians penetrated far into Gaul in 407, and some thrust on into Spain in 409, thus weakening communications between Rome and Britain, which was now dangerously isolated. The remaining forces in Britain, in default of help from Stilicho, elected three leaders in short succession. The first, Marcus (probably Count of Britain), was murdered almost as soon as he was chosen in 406. The second, Gratian, a native Briton, lasted only four months before being assassinated. The third, Constantine, also a Briton, survived for three years (407–11). Rightly or wrongly he decided to neglect the Picts and Scots, and believed that a threat of invasion from Gaul should be met by a pre-emptive strike. So, following the example of Magnus Maximus, he collected all the troops he could and crossed the Channel (407). Some successes in Gaul and Spain led the emperor Honorius to give him temporary recognition, but Constantine's British *magister militum*, Gerontius, rebelled in Spain and the barbarians gained the upper hand in Gaul. Before long the clash came, and Constantine had to surrender to Honorius who put him to death.

Meanwhile Britain, denuded of troops, had to face not only a hostile Gaul but also, if a Gallic chronicler of the mid-fifth century is to be believed, a large-scale Saxon invasion in 408. How she reacted is somewhat obscure: somehow the Saxons were kept at bay or defeated. According to the more general view, although their leader Constantine had taken up arms against the legitimate emperor, the Britons did not consider that they had opted out of the empire. In 410 they appealed to Honorius, but he could do nothing except order the native communities to arrange for their own defence as best they could: the raising of local forces would not be considered an act of rebellion against Rome. But mere authorization meant little: how was defence to be organized? There were no Counts or Dukes left, no *vicarii* or governors, no generals. The initiative was most probably taken by the upper class, the *curiales*, in support of the towns, acting perhaps through the old provincial council. An alternative view is that, while in 407 the Britons were merely putting forward their own leader as a rival to the emperor in Rome, in 409 they decided to rebel against Rome since Constantine could no longer defend them, thus obliging them to organize their own defence. This complete rejection of Rome is further interpreted by some as based on a social revolution, a 'peasant revolt' like that of the Bacaudae in Gaul. The peasantry successfully opposed the curial class, which appealed in vain to Honorius, and then they defeated the Saxons. However, whether or not the Britons rebelliously sought separation and independence from Rome, or were merely allowed to slip out of a distintegrating community, it seems hardly likely that the lower classes alone could have organized resistance to the Saxons; the initiative more probably came from the urbanized part of the community. When Germanus arrived in Britain in 429 there was no clear military leadership until he assumed it himself, but he did find at St Albans a *vir tribuniciae potestatis*, presumably a local magistrate in charge of the town, which indicates that some organized town life still survived.

However that may be, Britain now ceased to be part of the Roman empire. But there had been no dramatic 'departure of the Romans' in 410. In so far as there was a departure, it was the series of withdrawals of army units which culminated in that of Constantine in 407. Gildas, writing over a century later, confuses the picture by making a false distinction between 'Britons' and 'Romans'. Britain did not suddenly cease to be Roman in a cultural sense in 410, nor was everyday life transformed overnight. It became administratively independent, no money arrived to pay the troops, and as the barbarian tides swept higher over the island and the Continent, its links with the Roman world perforce gradually disintegrated. And for good, since the theory of a temporary Roman reoccupation of part of the island *c.* 417–25, based on an interpretation of the forces listed in the *Notitia Dignitatum*, is not now widely accepted.

Resistance to Saxon pressure was increased both by the presence of St Germanus and his 'Alleluia' victory, and also, paradoxically, by the spread of Pelagianism, the heresy he had been sent to Britain to combat. For even if this is not to be interpreted as a movement of social reform and is thought of as being rather more ascetic, Pelagius' emphasis on the power of human will and personal responsibility may have done much to hearten individual Britons. Furthermore, some local leaders emerged, especially in the west and north, including Vortigern (High King) whose rule began in 426. He strengthened North Wales against the Irish by arranging the migration of Cunedda and the Votadini from the Upper Tyne valley to North Wales, thus establishing the royal house of Gwynedd; this transfer, provided that it is fact rather than later legend, would seem to fit into place better in this context than earlier.

However his policy of hiring some Saxon mercenaries (traditionally led by Hengist and Horsa) to fight against renewed Pictish attacks, and then settling them in Kent (*c.* 430?) was dangerous. Furthermore, Vortigern was probably a Pelagian, so when Germanus tilted the balance against Pelagianism Vortigern's authority would have been weakened. It was the

Catholic bishops who had appealed to the Church in Gaul for help against Pelagianism, and so they would probably have been in part responsible for the last pathetic appeal to Aetius in Rome for military help in 446. That such an appeal was made is the one probable fact that emerges from a most confused passage of Gildas, who refers to three different appeals. Despite the plea that 'the barbarians drive us to the sea, and the sea drives us back to the barbarians: between these two forms of death we are either slaughtered or drowned,' no answer came.

The traditional date of the landing of the Saxons is that given by Bede, namely 448, but some had certainly been allowed to settle some 20 years earlier. Their arrival was preceded, according to Bede, by a period of prosperity and successes over the Picts and Irish until plague intervened and the Saxons rebelled, sweeping over southeast England with fire and sword, and destroying men and cities. Thus in the decades before the appeal to Aetius the decline had been very gradual. After Constantine III in 407 the supplies of new coinage ceased and the use of current coins, increasingly worn, gradually dwindled until, by 430, barter had replaced coinage. Many smaller potteries had gone out of business in the disturbances of 367, but those that survived probably did not outlast the 410s. The decline of villas and towns was even more gradual. Some villas were sacked, but the majority seem merely to have lapsed into decay, as labour became less reliable (some peasants turned to brigandage, others were at the mercy of plundering bands) and owners perhaps sought the safety of houses in the towns: some even seem to have tried to protect their villas by employing bands of federate German soldiers, whose characteristic bronze buckles have been found in a few villas. Yet the story of St Patrick, who returned home after being carried off by Irish raiders in his youth, shows that his father's villa (in the Bristol Channel area?) was still functioning c. 430. But by Gildas' time, about 100 years later, the villas had apparently disappeared. As regards the peasants, some merely stayed on – as probably did most of the inhabitants of the district around the Wall – but others fled westwards before the Saxon advance, some eventually even crossing to Brittany. In the west, especially in Wales, where the farmers had to face not only these refugees but also continued attacks by the Irish, there are signs of a move back into the old hillforts.

The fate of the towns naturally varied in different parts of the country. Their supposed decay from the middle of the fourth century must be rejected, and many survived into the fifth. But how much longer? The problem, however, is not primarily chronological, since *some* sort of life may have dragged on in many towns until the Middle Ages. Rather, it is a question of how long the towns survived as institutions, and whether there was any continuity of cultural life or of direct descent of the population from the earlier inhabitants. The answer in these terms appears to be that most of the towns had stopped functioning by, or before, the middle of the fifth century. At first they may have offered safe lodging for refugees from the countryside, since their fortified walls, manned at times by federate Germanic soldiers, could withstand attacks by the invading Saxons. But overcrowding may have led to famine since the villas could not longer supply the produce they needed, while pestilence may sometimes have followed. Indeed the view that intermittent plagues played a major part in the destruction of orderly life in the towns has recently been popular, but is unproved.

The archaeological evidence is sparse, but it points to some civilized life at least until *c.* 450 in Cirencester, Silchester and St Albans, though it would probably be going too far to think in terms of a Celtic revival. The worn floor of the forum at Cirencester appears to have been kept clean and in use until *c.* 430, but afterwards a newly dug drainage ditch was allowed to fill up with grass and weeds. In another ditch two human bodies were found, so by that time grass was growing in the streets and unburied bodies were allowed to rot in ditches beside the road. At Silchester, fifth-century beads and glass have been found, and a column, inscribed in Ogham script and belonging to *c.* 450 or considerably later, suggests the presence of Celtic inhabitants. St Albans provides more evidence. There a fine mosaic floor was cut through to allow the insertion of a corn-drying oven (*c.* 430?): with the countryside unsettled it was important to avoid delay in collecting the harvest, and, to dry it in safety. Later the building was demolished and replaced by a barn, which survived until *c.* 460, when a wooden water-pipe was laid across the site: the town's water supply, and the skill necessary for its upkeep, apparently still survived. In general, the further east the towns lay, the quicker they probably succumbed to the Saxons, with Canterbury, London, Colchester and Lincoln among the first to disappear, while some life survived in Wroxeter until the late fifth century. Those former Roman towns which flourished in the Middle Ages and later owed their success to the excellence of their sites rather than to any tenuous continuation of life on the spot: a few squatters amid decayed buildings do not make a town. The representatives of Romano-British culture had long either fled or died out. One of the greatest gifts brought to Britain by the Romans was urbanization: now cut off from its Roman roots, town life withered and died.

Brief list of events

BC

c. 125–75   Belgic tribes from the Continent spread into southeast Britain.

55   Julius Caesar's first attack on southeast Britain.

54   Caesar's second invasion, defeat of Cassivellaunus in Hertfordshire and conquest of southeast Britain.

54 BC–AD 43   Britain left in peace by Rome. Increasing trade contacts. The Atrebates (capital at Silchester) consolidate under Commius, his son Tincommius (c. 25/20 BC–AD 5/6), who flees to Augustus, Eppillus (c. AD 6–?), and Verica (?–AD 43), who flees to Claudius.
The Catuvellauni: Cassivellaunus reigns till c. 20 BC. He is succeeded by Tasciovanus, followed in c. AD 5 by Cunobelinus, who makes Colchester his capital, and expands and consolidates his kingdom. Quarrel with his son Adminius who flees to emperor Claudius. Cunobelinus succeeded (c. AD 40/41) by Togidumnus and Caratacus who expels Verica.

AD

40   Caligula's abortive threat to Britain.

43   Claudian invasion of Britain. Capture of Colchester. Britannia a Roman province.

43–47   The governor Aulus Plautius extends occupation to the Severn and Wash; establishes good relations with the Regni, Iceni and Brigantes beyond the province.

47–52   Ostorius Scapula disarms all tribes south of the Fosse Way, checks the Silures (legionary base at Kingsholme, Gloucester) and Brigantes, and defeats Caratacus (51). Roman colony at Colchester.

c. 55–60   Legio IX established at Lincoln.

58–59   Suetonius Paulinus campaigns in South Wales.

60   Suetonius defeats Deceangli, and the Druids in Anglesey. Revolt of the Iceni under Boudicca.

Sack of Colchester, London and St Albans. Defeat of Boudicca. Suetonius superseded.

71   Petilius Cerealis moves Legio IX from Lincoln to York and defeats Brigantes under Venutius.

74–78   Sextus Julius Frontinus governor. He moves Legio II from Gloucester to Caerleon, defeats the Silures and attacks the Ordovices; establishes many forts and roads in Wales. Legio II Adiutrix at Chester (c. 78).

78–84   Agricola defeats the Ordovices (78) and Brigantes, and reaches the Tyne–Solway (79), occupies Scottish Lowlands (80), consolidates and builds roads and forts (81), turns to southwest Scotland (82), advances into the Highlands with legionary fortress at Inchtuthil (83), defeats the Caledonians at Mons Graupius (84). Recalled to Rome (84–85).
Romanization and urbanization of Britain promoted by Agricola. Growing importance of London and other towns, including tribal capitals (*civitates*).

c. 87   Highlands of Scotland abandoned; frontier along Clyde–Forth line.

c. 90–98   Roman colonies at Lincoln (c. 90) and Gloucester (c. 96–98).

c. 105   Lowlands of Scotland abandoned. New frontier under Trajan along the Stanegate (Tyne–Solway line).

c. 118   Revolt among the Brigantes suppressed.

122   Hadrian visits Britain. Legio VI Victrix replaces IX Hispana. Building of Hadrian's Wall started, under Platorius Nepos.

139   Reoccupation of southern Scotland and building of Antonine Wall started.

150–160   Sometime in decade revolt in north Britain crushed. Antonine Wall temporarily evacuated, but soon reoccupied c. 158–163.

c. 163   More trouble in north and final abandonment of Antonine Wall. Hadrian's Wall strengthened.

180　Tribes from north overrun the Wall (presumably Hadrian's).

184　Invaders crushed by Ulpius Marcellus, but frontier fixed at Hadrian's Wall.

c. 191　Clodius Albinus governor of Britain.

193　Clodius claims the imperial throne, is temporarily recognized by Septimius Severus, and strengthens some British towns with earth ramparts.

196　Clodius crosses to France, denuding Britain of troops. Northern tribes break through Hadrian's Wall.

197　Clodius defeated and killed by Septimius Severus.

197–202　Virius Lupus, governor, restores situation in north Britain. Britain divided into two provinces, Superior and Inferior.

205–207　Alfenius Senecio, governor, restores Hadrian's Wall and forts.

208–209　Septimius Severus, the emperor, arrives in Britain and advances to near Aberdeen.

211　Septimius dies at York. Scotland evacuated, and Hadrian's Wall remains the frontier.

212　Caracalla grants Roman citizenship to nearly all the Roman empire, including Britain.

c. 217–270　Britain peaceful. Much rebuilding. Towns provided with stone walls.

259–273　Britain part of an independent empire based on France.

c. 275　Increase of Saxon raids on southeast British coasts. Most of the forts of the Saxon Shore built about this time (? by Probus, 276–282).

286–287　Carausius, naval commander in the English Channel, establishes an independent rule in Britain and northern France.

293/4　Carausius murdered by Allectus, who succeeds him in Britain.

293　Diocletian's reorganization of the Roman empire; Britain becomes one of twelve dioceses under a vicar; divided into four provinces. The office of *Dux Britanniarum*, commander of forces, stationed at York, probably established now.

296　Constantius (Caesar) defeats Allectus and recovers Britain; perhaps campaigns in Scotland and begins repairing damage to Hadrian's Wall.

306　Constantius returns to Britain, as emperor, and campaigns in Scotland. Dies at York, where his son Constantine is proclaimed emperor. Constantine, before leaving, carries out reconstruction in Britain, which enters a period of peace and prosperity till c. 342. Office of Count of the Saxon Shore perhaps established now.

313　Christianity recognized throughout the empire.

314　Three British bishops at the Council of Arles.

342–343　Disturbances north of Hadrian's Wall.

343　Emperor Constans visits Britain and restores position. Office of Count of the Saxon Shore established now, if not earlier.

350–353　Britain deprived of more troops by Magnentius in his abortive usurpation of the Roman empire.

360　Picts and Scots, ravaging territory north of the Wall, are contained by Lupicinus, sent by emperor Julian. Julian's pagan reaction to Christianity encourages paganism in British countryside till end of century, but temples gradually decline, first in towns, then in country.

367　Britain invaded by a great barbarian 'conspiracy' of Picts, Scots and Saxons. Hadrian's Wall overrun, Count of Saxon Shore and Duke of Britain crushed.

369　Valentinian sends Count Theodosius, who restores order. Wall restored, forts rebuilt and signal stations established on Yorkshire coast. Town walls provided with bastions. This reconstruction gives both towns and villas peace and prosperity for at least a quarter of a century.

383　North Britain again threatened by Picts and Scots. Magnus Maximus, probably Duke of Britain, elected emperor by army in Britain, withdraws troops to fight (successfully until 388) on the Continent. But Hadrian's Wall probably still held.

395　Roman empire formally divided into two parts, East and West.

396–398　Stilicho, general of young emperor Honorius, campaigns against seaborne invasions of Scots, Picts and Saxons.

c. 400	End of Hadrian's Wall.		429	St Germanus sent to Britain to combat Pelagianism; he defeats Picts and Saxons in the 'Alleluia victory'. St Ninian (d. *c.* 432) active as Christian missionary in Scotland, and St Patrick in Ireland (431–461).

c. 400   End of Hadrian's Wall.

401   Troops withdrawn from Britain to defend Italy against the Visigoth Alaric.

406   Britons elect Marcus, who is quickly murdered, and then Gratian.

407   Constantine III, successor to Gratian, crosses to Continent with all the troops he can muster. Burgundians penetrate far into France and (409) into Spain, thus weakening communications between Rome and Britain.

408   Probable Saxon invasion of Britain.

410   Britons appeal for help to emperor Honorius, who tells them to arrange their own defence.

c. 417–435   A temporary Roman reoccupation of Britain very improbable.

c. 426   Emergence of some local leaders, such as Vortigern, in west and north.

429   St Germanus sent to Britain to combat Pelagianism; he defeats Picts and Saxons in the 'Alleluia victory'. St Ninian (d. *c.* 432) active as Christian missionary in Scotland, and St Patrick in Ireland (431–461).

430–446   Decline of towns and villas very gradual. Barter replaces money by 430. According to Bede, some prosperity and successes in the 20 years before 448 (his date for the main Saxon landing).

446   Last appeal by Britons to Aetius, the effective ruler of the Western empire.

450   Civilized life in most towns has now disappeared, but a shadow lingers on briefly in a few. Disappearance, under Saxon pressure, of Celtic culture, language and religion in England, but survival of Celtic Church and British-Celtic tongue in highland areas.

SOME OF THE ROMAN EMPERORS

Augustus	BC 27–AD 14	Hadrian	117–138	Diocletian	284–305
Tiberius	AD 14–37	Antoninus Pius	138–161	Constantius	292–306
Caligula	37–41	M. Aurelius	161–180	Constantine	306–337
Claudius	41–54	Commodus	180–192	Constans	337–350
Nero	54–68	Septimius Severus	193–211	Julian	360–363
Vespasian	69–79	Caracalla	211–217	Valentinian I	364–375
Titus	79–81	Decius	249–251	Theodosius I	378–395
Domitian	81–96	Aurelian	270–275	Honorius	395–423
Trajan	98–117	Probus	276–282		

Further reading

General

BIRLEY, A. *Life in Roman Britain*, London, 1964.

COLLINGWOOD, R.G., and J.N.L. MYRES *Roman Britain and the English settlements*, Oxford, 1936.

FRERE, S.S. *Britannia*, London, 1978.

LIVERSIDGE, J. *Britain in the Roman Empire*, London, 1968.

RICHMOND, I.A. *Roman Britain* (revised edition), London, 1963.

WACHER, J. *Roman Britain*, London, 1978.

Special aspects

CHADWICK, N. *The Celts*, Harmondsworth, 1970.

COLLINGWOOD, R.G., and I.A. RICHMOND *The Archaeology of Roman Britain* (revised edition), London, 1969.

DOBSON, B., and D.J. BREEZE *Hadrian's Wall*, Durham, 1976.

LEWIS, M.J.P. *Temples in Roman Britain*, London, 1966.

MARGARY, I.D. *Roman Roads in Britain* (revised edition), London, 1967.

NASH WILLIAMS, V.E. *The Roman Frontier in Wales* (revised edition), Cardiff, 1969.

POWELL, T.G. *The Celts*, London, 1965.

RIVET, A.L. *Town and Country in Roman Britain* (revised edition), London, 1966.

RIVET, A.L. (editor) *The Roman Villa in Britain*, London, 1969.

SALWAY, P. *The Frontier People of Roman Britain*, Cambridge, 1965.

TOYNBEE, J.M.C. *Art in Britain under the Romans*, Oxford, 1964.

WACHER, J. *The Towns of Roman Britain*, London, 1975.

WEBSTER, G. *Boudicca*, London, 1978.

WILSON, R.J.A. *Roman Remains in Britain*, London, 1975.

Sources

The ancient literary sources are usefully collected and edited in R.W. Moore, *The Romans in Britain* (third edition), London, 1954, and (in English) in *The Literary Sources for Roman Britain*, edited by J.C. Mann and R.G. Penman (*Lactor*, no. 11, London Association of Classical Teachers, 19b Roxborough Park, Harrow, Middx, published 1977). Good selections of inscriptions are given with commentary by A.R. Burn, *The Romans in Britain* (revised edition), Oxford, 1969, and *Some Inscriptions from Roman Britain* (*Lactor*, no. 4). The standard collection of all inscriptions of Roman Britain is R.G. Collingwood and R.P. Wright, *Roman Inscriptions of Britain*, I, Oxford, 1965. A detailed annual report of archaeological finds in Roman Britain is given each year (from 1970) in the periodical *Britannia* (for earlier annual reviews see *Journal of Roman Studies*).

References to inscriptions

Burn: A. R. Burn, *The Romans in Britain* (1969).
CIL: *Corpus Inscriptionum Latinarum*.
ILS: *Inscriptiones Latinae Selectae*, by H. Dessau.
JRS: *Journal of Roman Studies*.
RIB: *The Roman Inscriptions of Britain*, I, by R. G. Collingwood and R. P. Wright.

page

39 Arch, Burn, 1.
 Antioch, BM Papyrus, 1178.
 Gavius, *ILS*, 2701.
 Anicius, *ILS*, 2696.
50 Cogidubnus, *RIB*, 91.
53 Agricola, Burn, 40.
55 Tombstones, *RIB*, 11, 13, 17, (Celsus) 19.
56 Lead pigs, *ILS*, 8709; Burn, 12; *CIL*, vii, 1201 ff.
72 Favonius, *RIB*, 200.
 Valens, *ILS*, 2648.
75 Virilis, Burn, 74.
 Rufus, *RIB*, 121.
76 Diploma, *ILS*, 2735; Burn, 95.
 Benwell, *RIB*, 1340.
 Lympne, *RIB*, 66.
 Maenius, *ILS*, 2735; Burn, 88; *RIB*, 823–6.
 Dover, *Britannia*, 1971, 286; 1972, 351; 1977, 235 ff.
79 Armatura, *RIB*, 305.
83 Centurial stones, *RIB*, 1813, 1816.
 Wine, references in R. W. Davies, *Britannia*, 1971, 122 ff.
 Vindolanda, A. K. Bowman, *Britannia*, 1974, 360 ff.

86 Victor, *RIB*, 1724.
 Bannienses, *RIB*, 1905.
 Veturius, *RIB*, 1041.
87 Iavolenus, *ILS*, 1015; Burn, 87.
88 Procurators, *BM Guide to Antiquities of Rom. Brit.* (1958), 48.
 Statilius, *ILS*, 9012.
 Censitor, *ILS*, 2740.
 Nepos, *ILS*, 1338.
90 Bellator, *RIB*, 674.
 Gloucester, *RIB*, 161.
 Lunaris, *JRS*, xi (1921).
 Memor, *JRS*, lvii; Burn, 82.
 Civitas Cornoviorum, *RIB*, 288.
 Civitas Petuaria, *RIB*, 707.
109 Julinus, *RIB*, 343.
 Retiarius, *Eboracum* (R.C.H.M., 1962), 135, no. 149.
 Verecunda, Burn, 55.
133 Goldsmith, *RIB*, 712.
134 Agricola, Burn, 27.
137 Tilery, *Archaeologia*, lix, 366.
 Gloucester, *Ephemeris Epigraphica*, iv, 699; ix, 1283.
142 Lunaris, Burn, 65.
 Diogenes, *RIB*, 678.
 Solinarius, *CIL*, xii, 634; Burn, 66.
 Placidus, *Britannia*, 1977, 430.
 Salmanes, *RIB*, 2182.
 Barates, *RIB*, 1065, 1171.
143 Isis, Burn, 53.
 Crescens, Burn, 46–8.
144 Rufus, Burn, 49.
 Graffiti, Burn, 52, 54–61.
 Dover, *Britannia*, 1973, 332.
 Hermogenes, *RIB*, 461.
 Lanchester, *RIB*, 1072.
 Chester, *RIB*, 443.

South Shields, etc., *RIB*, 1052, 808.
145 Prescriptions, Burn, 80; *Britannia*, 1977, 435.
 Stolus, *Britannia*, 1977, 279 ff.
149 Cunorix, *JRS*, 1968, 206 ff.
153 Priscus, *RIB*, 149.
 Sulinus, *RIB*, 151.
155 Lunaris, Burn, 65.
156 Brough (Petuaria), *RIB*, 707.
 Colchester, *RIB*, 193.
 Cogidubnus, *RIB*, 81.
 Maryport, *RIB*, 823.
 Newstead, *RIB*, 2123.
 Housesteads, *RIB*, 1591, 1580.
 Sextianus, *RIB*, 946.
 Pantera, *RIB*, 66.
 Tynemouth, *RIB*, 1319.
 Newstead, *RIB*, 2120.
 Vindolanda, *RIB*, 1700.
157 Celatus, *RIB*, 274.
 Victoria, *RIB*, 2144.
 British victory, *ILS*, 436; Burn, 197.
 Brigantia, *RIB*, 1131.
158 Mars Cocidius, *RIB*, 2044.
 Thincsus, *RIB*, 1595.
159 Nodens, *RIB*, 306.
160 Curses, *RIB*, 6, 7.
161 Coventina, *RIB*, 1534.
164 Isis, Burn, 53; *Britannia*, 1976, 378 ff.
 Serapis, *RIB*, 658.
165 Astarte, *RIB*, 1124.
166 Spes, etc., Burn, 226.
167 Water Newton, *Britannia*, 1976, 385.
168 Giant column, *RIB*, 103.
173 Carvoran, *RIB*, 1843.

List of Illustrations

Rough Castle, Antonine Wall. Photo Crown copyright, reproduced by permission of the Department of the Environment.

64 Cavalry parade helmet, from Ribchester, Lancs. British Museum, London.

66 Roman fort, Richborough, Kent. Photo Cambridge University Collection, copyright reserved.

67 Porchester Castle, Hants., air view from the southeast. Photo Department of the Environment, Crown copyright.

68 *Denarius* of Marcus Aurelius Carausius. Obverse, head of Carausius. British Museum, London.

70 Soldiers building a wall. From Trajan's Column, Rome. Photo Mansell-Alinari.

73 Inscribed funerary *stele* of Marcus Favonius Facilis, centurion of Legio XX at Colchester. Colchester and Essex Museum, Colchester.

74 Tombstone of a trooper of a Thracian *ala*. Corinium Museum, Cirencester.

75 Roman military diploma from Dacia showing British units. Muzeul de Istoria Cluz, Romania. From G.R. Watson, *The Roman Soldier*, Pl. 10, Thames and Hudson, London, 1969.

76 Dover lighthouse (*pharos*). Photo Department of the Environment, Crown copyright.

77 Roman galley. Science Museum, London.

78 Bronze centreplate of a legionary's shield. Found in the river Tyne. British Museum, London.

79 Models of a legionary and a praetorian. Museo della Civiltà Romana, Rome. Photo Alinari.

80 Plan of unfinished legionary fortress at Inchtuthil, Perthshire. From R.G. Collingwood and I.A. Richmond, *The Archaeology of Roman Britain*, Methuen, London, 1969.

81 Plan of legionary fortress at Caerleon, Gwent. From R.G. Collingwood and I.A. Richmond, *The Archaeology of Roman Britain*, Methuen & Co. Ltd, London, 1969.

82 Roman soldiers making a road. From Trajan's Column, Rome. Photo Alinari.

84 Two leaves of a writing-tablet. Before AD 105. From Vindolanda, Northumberland. The Vindolanda Trust. Photo R. Birley.

85 A *medicus* attending a wounded soldier. From Trajan's Column, Rome. Photo Deutsches Archaeologisches Institut, Rome.

86 A stone gaming-board. From Vindolanda, Northumberland. The Vindolanda Trust. Photo R. Birley.

87 Writing tablet with the official procuratorial stamp. British Museum, London.

90 Inscription from entrance to the forum, Wroxeter, Shropshire. Dedicated to Hadrian by *civitas* of Cornovii, AD 131. From R.G. Collingwood and R.P. Wright, *Roman Inscriptions of Britain*, Vol. 1, published by Oxford University Press, 1965.

95 Southern defensive wall, Caerwent, late 2nd century AD. Photo National Museum of Wales, Cardiff

Reconstruction drawing of Caerwent. Photo National Museum of Wales, Cardiff.

96 Plan of Roman city of London. After R. Merrifield. From J. Wacher, *Towns of Roman Britain*, B.T. Batsford Ltd, London, 1975.

98 Crop marks showing Roman town, Silchester, Hants. Photo Cambridge University Collection, copyright reserved.

St Albans (Verulamium). 4th century. After S.S. Frere. From J. Wacher, *Towns of Roman Britain*, B.T. Batsford Ltd, London, 1975.

99 Reconstruction of forum and basilica at Silchester from the northeast. From George C. Boon, *Roman Silchester*, Max Parrish, London, 1957.

100 The *mansio* (roadhouse) at Godmanchester, Cambridgeshire. Reconstruction drawing by H.J.M. Green, *Arch. Newsletter*, VI.

101 Reconstruction of Romano-British temple, Silchester. From George C. Boon, *Roman Silchester*, Max Parrish, London, 1957.

Roman temple, Maiden Castle, Dorset. Photo R.J.A. Wilson.

102 Plan of public baths, Silchester. From George C. Boon, *Roman Silchester*, Max Parrish, London, 1957.

103 Roman baths, Bath, Avon.

104 Part of a bronze Roman waterpump. British Museum, London.

105 Roman theatre of St Albans (Verulamium). Photo Aerofilms.

The theatre, Verulamium. Reconstruction drawing by Alan Sorrell. Verulamium Museum, St Albans.

106 Mosaic pavement with chariot scenes. From Horkstow, Lincs. British Museum, London.

108 Amphitheatre at Caerleon, *c.* AD 80. Photo Aerofilms.

Roman gladiator vase. Colchester and Essex Museum, Colchester.

109 Jet bear. Colchester and Essex Museum, Colchester.

110 Reconstruction of House I, Insula XXIII, Silchester. From George C. Boon, *Roman Silchester*, Max Parrish, London, 1957.

114 Reconstruction of villa at Lockleys, Welwyn, Herts. Drawing by H. C. Lander. From J.B. Ward-Perkins, 'The Roman Villa at Lockleys', *Antiquity*, XIV (1940).

Plan of villa at Lockleys, Welwyn, Herts. From J.B. Ward-Perkins, 'The Roman Villa at Lockleys', *Antiquity*, XIV (1940).

115 Plan of villa at Ditchley, Oxon. *Oxoniensia*, Vol. 1, 1936, by permission of *Oxoniensia* and C.A. Raleigh Radford.

116 Plan of courtyard villa, North Leigh, Oxon. After D.R. Wilson. From A.L. Rivet (ed.), *The Roman Villa in Britain*, Routledge and Kegan Paul, London, 1969.

117 Reconstruction of villa at Chedworth, near Cirencester, *c*. AD 300. After Ward-Perkins.

Plan of villa at Chedworth. After Richmond. From A.L. Rivet (ed.), *The Roman Villa in Britain*, Routledge and Kegan Paul, London, 1969.

118 Villa and farmyard at Llantwit Major, Glamorgan. Reconstruction drawing by Alan Sorrell. Photo National Museum of Wales, Cardiff.

119 Palace at Fishbourne, Sussex. Isometric drawing by David S. Neal.

120 Villa with temple mausoleum and circular temple, Lullingstone, Kent. Reconstruction drawing by Alan Sorrell. Photo Department of the Environment, Crown copyright.

121 Mosaic of the Rape of Europa, Lullingstone villa, Kent. Photo Department of the Environment, Crown copyright.

Christian wall painting. From Lullingstone villa, Kent. British Museum, London.

122 Banqueting scene from a tombstone. Found at Kirkby Thore, Northumberland. British Museum, London.

124 Silver dish. Early 4th century. From Mildenhall, Suffolk. British Museum, London.

126 Roman iron knives and saws. Museum of London.

127 Bronze dog. Found near temple of Nodens at Lydney, Glos. Private collection.

Jar with hunting scene. Nene Valley ware. British Museum, London.

130 Wooden water-wheel. British Museum, London.

132 Grave relief of a blacksmith. Yorkshire Museum, York.

134 Glass flagon, from Bayford, Kent. British Museum, London.

135 Shallow bowl. Samian ware. British Museum, London.

136 Castor ware beaker with chariot race. From Colchester, Essex. British Museum, London.

Indented beaker. New Forest ware. British Museum, London.

139 Roman roadway, Wheeldale Moor, Yorks. Photo R.J.A. Wilson.

Cross-section of Roman road.

140 Relief showing mules drawing a cart. From the Igel monument, near Trier. Photo Landesmuseum, Trier.

141 Gold medallion of Constantius I, AD 296 (the Arras medal).

142 Silver-fir wine barrels. Found at Silchester. His Grace the Duke of Wellington's Loan Collection at Reading Museum. Photo Reading Museum and Art Gallery.

143 Tombstone of Regina, British wife of a Palmyrean businessman. Found

at South Shields. Roman Fort and Museum, South Shields.

146 Male hunter deity in oolitic limestone. Found in a late Roman well below Southwark cathedral, excavated in 1977. Southwark and Lambeth Archaeological Excavation Committee.

152 Medusa head. From the temple of Minerva, Bath. Roman Baths Museum, Bath.

Head of Constantine. 4th century. From York. Photo Warburg Institute, University of London.

Roman head of Antenociticus. From Benwell, Northumberland. The Museum of Antiquities of the University, and the Society of Antiquaries, Newcastle upon Tyne.

153 Stone carving of a lion. From Corbridge, Northumberland. Corbridge Museum. Photo Department of the Environment, Crown copyright.

Statue of Juno Regina. From Chesters, Northumberland. Chesters Museum. Photo Warburg Institute, University of London.

155 Reconstruction of the temple of Claudius at Colchester. From J. Wacher, *Roman Britain*, J. M. Dent, London, 1978.

157 Sculptured block with head of Mars. Found in Upper Thames Street, Baynards Castle site, excavated in 1975. Photo T.J. Hurst, Museum of London.

158 Plaque of three deities. Found at Housesteads, Northumberland. Housesteads Museum. Photo Department of the Environment, Crown copyright.

159 Stone-relief dedicated to the goddess Brigantia. From Dumfriesshire. National Museum of Antiquities in Scotland, Edinburgh.

161 Stone dedicated to the water goddess, Coventina. 2nd–3rd century. From Carrawburgh, Northumberland. Photo Warburg Institute, University of London.

162 Mithraic relief. Late 3rd century. Museum of London.

163 Temple of Mithras, Carrawburgh, Northumberland. Photo R.J.A. Wilson.

165 Head of Serapis. Late 2nd century. From the Walbrook Mithraeum. Museum of London.

166 Silver strainer with Chi-Rho. 4th century. From the Water Newton treasure. British Museum, London.

168 Floor mosaic showing Christ and other figures. 4th century. From Hinton St Mary, Dorset. Photo National Monuments Record.

169 Christian church, Silchester. After W.H. St John Hope. From J. Wacher, *Roman Britain*, J. M. Dent, London, 1978.

170 Forts of the Saxon Shore. A late medieval copy of a page from the 5th-century *Notitia Dignitatum*. Bodleian Library, Oxford.

172 Bronze *maiorina* of Magnentius, AD 350–3. Obverse, head of Magnentius. British Museum, London.

174 Gold *solidus* of Magnus Maximus, AD 383–8. Obverse, head of Magnus Maximus. British Museum, London.

Index